"*As a long-time Las Vegas resident and retired Senior Agent of the Nevada Gaming Control Board, I can state that Dennis Griffin has put together the real story of the Spilotro years in Vegas.*"

—Jack Miller

❖

"*Wow ... Dennis Griffin has really captured the Las Vegas I knew; it's an amazing book. If you want to know about Las Vegas in the mob days, this book says it all. It's a great read.*"

—Tru Hawkins
Long-time Las Vegan and host of the "Tru Hawkins Show" on KDWN Radio

❖

"*There has been a lot written and filmed about the days when the mob reigned in Las Vegas, mostly from the point of view of the mobsters and their attorneys. In* The Battle for Las Vegas, *Dennis Griffin has added balance by including the law-enforcement side of things. If you want to know the true story of what it was really like back then, you need to read this book.*"

—Lt. Gene Smith (retired)
Las Vegas Metropolitan Police Department

❖

"*Finally, a book about the mob in Las Vegas from the law-enforcement perspective. Dennis Griffin has thoroughly researched and accurately written the story about how law enforcement fought and won the battle to rid Las Vegas of the influence and control of organized crime. It was a pleasure to live through those times again in the pages of this book.*"

—Dennis Arnoldy (retired)
FBI case agent for the Spilotro investigations in Las Vegas

The Battle for Las Vegas

Other Books by Dennis N. Griffin

The Morgue

Red Gold

Blood Money

Killer In Pair-A-Dice

One-Armed Bandit

Pension

Policing Las Vegas

Cullotta

The Battle for Las Vegas

The Law vs. The Mob

Dennis N. Griffin

Huntington Press
Las Vegas, Nevada

The Battle for Las Vegas
The Law vs. The Mob

Published by
Huntington Press
3665 Procyon Ave.
Las Vegas, NV 89103
Phone (702) 252-0655
e-mail: books@huntingtonpress.com

Copyright ©2006, Dennis N. Griffin

ISBN: 0-929712-37-4

Cover Design: Laurie Shaw
Interior Design & Production: Laurie Shaw

Photo credits: Dennis Arnoldy, Mike Bunker, Kent Clifford, Jim Erbeck, Lynn Ferrin, Dennis N. Griffin, Tru Hawkins, Gary Magnesen, John McCarthy, Gene Smith, Illinois Department of Corrections, *Las Vegas Review-Journal*, Las Vegas Metropolitian Police Department, Office of Mayor Goodman, UNLV Special Collections

Dedication

This book is dedicated to the men and women of law enforcement, sworn and civilian, whose diligence and professionalism make us all more safe and secure. The battles they fight on our behalf—often at great personal risk—warrant our sincerest gratitude.

Acknowledgments

I want to express my heartfelt gratitude to all those current and former law-enforcement personnel who shared their experiences, insights, photos, and time in helping me write this book. They include, but are not limited to, former Clark County Sheriff John McCarthy, Commander Kent Clifford, Detective David Groover and Lt. Gene Smith, former Deputy District Attorney Jim Erbeck, former Strike Force Special Attorney Stanley Hunterton, and former FBI agents Joe Yablonsky, Charlie Parsons, Emmett Michaels, Dennis Arnoldy, Lynn Ferrin, and Gary Magnesen.

The newspaper archives of the Las Vegas–Clark County Library District held stories from the *Las Vegas Sun*, *The Valley Times*, and *Las Vegas Review-Journal* that provided key information regarding events and incidents of the era I was researching. A series of 1983 articles by Michael Goodman of the *Los Angeles Times* proved to be equally beneficial.

The well-researched books *The Green Felt Jungle* (Reid and Demaris), *Of Rats and Men* (John L. Smith), and *The First 100* (A.D. Hopkins and K.J. Evans) provided crucial background information into the history of organized crime's influence in Las Vegas. I also watched the movie *Casino*—in which actors Joe Pesci and Robert De Niro portrayed characters based on Tony Spilotro and Frank "Lefty" Rosenthal—numerous times.

Three former casino insiders, whom I call Sammy, Mario, and Mickey, gave me a feel for what it was like in the gaming establishments and on the Strip during the Spilotro years. A woman, "Connie," who was employed by the Argent Corporation at that time and worked directly for Frank Rosenthal, shared her memories with me. Tru Hawkins of KDWN Radio and a life-long resident of Las Vegas offered his perceptions of those days, as well.

A bartender, "Joe," who worked in several Las Vegas clubs and casinos during Spilotro's reign, offered further insights into the atmosphere of Las Vegas during the days of mob control. "Harry," a veteran Sin City bail bondsman, provided ideas of how information of law-enforcement activities made its way to the bad guys.

Veteran newsman Bob Stoldal of KLAS-TV, Gwen Castaldi, former KLAS reporter, Andrea Boggs, former KVBC-TV anchor and reporter, and Jane Ann Morrison of the *Las Vegas Review-Journal* provided a look at the Spilotro years from the media perspective.

I also extend my thanks to Nancy and Vincent Spilotro, Tony's widow and son, for helping out with personal insights about their husband and father.

There are many others who deserve mention, but for various legitimate reasons desire to be anonymous. Respecting their wishes, they will remain nameless, but not unappreciated.

Contents

Introduction

Las Vegas and its ties to organized crime are well-known, the subject of many books, TV documentaries, and movies. In my previous book, *Policing Las Vegas—A History of Law Enforcement in Southern Nevada*, I wrote a section called "The Mob's Man," concerning the Las Vegas reign of Tony Spilotro, a made man of the Chicago crime family.

Tony and his wife Nancy, both 33 years old at the time, and their five-year-old son Vincent moved to Las Vegas in 1971. Known as a tough and ruthless gangland enforcer, Spilotro allegedly used intimidation, and sometimes murder, to protect Chicago's criminal interests in Vegas until his own death in 1986. When he wasn't acting directly on the Chicago family's behalf, law enforcement believed that Tony ran a gang that committed lucrative street crimes, including loan sharking, robbery, burglary, and fencing stolen goods. Eventually his status required that he be paid a "street tax"—a kickback—from other criminal groups wanting to operate their own illegal enterprises. The word was that nothing happened in Vegas—from loan sharking to contract killings—without Tony's knowledge and blessing.

The deeper I dug, the more intrigued I became with Tony Spilotro and the battle the law waged against him and his gang. It was a fight with tough men on both sides. I gathered enough information to complete that section of the book, but knew I'd only scratched the surface of the story.

Another area that captured my attention while writing *Policing Las Vegas* was the term of Sheriff John McCarthy. He won election as a reform candidate in 1978, defeating 17-year incumbent Ralph Lamb. However, his term in office was controversial and chaotic. Even before assuming office in January 1979, Sheriff McCarthy was sued by a group of Metro officers for announcing the promotions of several detectives and patrolmen to upper-management positions, over others with more rank, service time, and experience. That rocky start set the stage for what were the most divisive four years in Metro's brief history.

A review of newspaper articles, records, and interviews with those who knew and worked for McCarthy revealed to me the almost daily turmoil that dogged his term. There were major problems with the jail, an attempt to deconsolidate Metro, and allegations of discrimination, abuse of power by his officers, and corruption within the department. All this was followed by a nasty election campaign in which the incumbent was challenged by his former undersheriff, whom he'd once fired. For Sheriff McCarthy and Metro, these were indeed turbulent times.

What particularly intrigued me about those four years, however, was the juxtaposition of the McCarthy era and the Spilotro reign. One of the first things McCarthy did after being sworn in was to declare war on organized crime. He wanted Tony Spilotro and his kind run out of town, making it one of his priorities. At the same time, the FBI and a Department of Justice Strike Force were increasing the pressure on Spilotro and his men. The battle was joined; the law was after the bad guys.

It was a tale I wanted to tell. But would I be able to make it interesting and informative, rather than simply regurgitate the same stories written over the years? I decided that if I could locate the local and federal lawmen who had actually fought the battles, as well as others in the know, and get them to participate, I'd be able to produce a book that would be satisfying to the reader, perhaps plowing some new ground in the process.

After a few initial disappointments in my search for sources, my luck changed. The list of those willing to cooperate began to grow. In a relatively short time, I was satisfied that I'd find sufficient material to move forward with the project.

I decided early on to concentrate on Spilotro's alleged street-crime activities, with the well-publicized casino skimming operations receiving somewhat less attention. Then, near the beginning of my research, I learned that Tony had no direct involvement in the skim—except in enforcement matters—and probably didn't even know the identities of the couriers who delivered the purloined cash to Chicago. Therefore, the discussion of those financial crimes is primarily limited to one section of this book.

The secondary focus of this endeavor is on the term of Sheriff McCarthy and the many wars he fought in addition to the one against organized crime. It's my hope that the stories go hand in hand and meld together well.

Our journey starts with a brief history of Las Vegas. We then explore organized-crime's early involvement there, starting with Ben "Bugsy" Siegel and the Flamingo Hotel and Casino. After that is some background on the key figures of the Chicago La Cosa Nostra (LCN) of Tony's days, the men who sent him to Las Vegas. Next I look at the early lives of Spilotro and his erstwhile pal, Frank "Lefty" Rosenthal. From there we move on to Tony's era in Las Vegas and the law's efforts to remove him.

Denny Griffin

1

The Early Years

In 1829, an 18-year-old Mexican scout for the Antonio Armijo Trading Caravan was tasked with finding a new trade route from Santa Fe, New Mexico, to Los Angeles. In his search he came upon an oasis in the desert. With abundant wild grasses and an ample water supply, it was a perfect place for the traders to stop and rest during their arduous journey. His discovery was named Las Vegas, which means The Meadows, but knowledge of its existence remained primarily limited to the Mexicans and the indigenous Paiute population until explorer John Frémont put it on the map in 1844.

In 1855, Brigham Young ordered 30 missionaries to Las Vegas Valley to build a fort and teach the Paiutes farming techniques. The Paiutes rejected the Mormon's offerings and the fort was abandoned in 1858. The area remained sparsely settled until the arrival of the railroad.

In the summer of 1904, work on the first railroad grade into Las Vegas began. Thanks to the water supply, a town sprouted, consisting of saloons, stores, and boarding houses to accommodate the railroad workers. On May 15, 1905, the railroad auctioned off 1,200 lots in a 40-block area surrounding downtown and Las Vegas was established as an unincorporated city. In 1909, it became the county seat for the new Clark County.

Railroaders were a hard drinking rough-and-tumble lot. The main problem the lawmen in those early days had to confront was dealing with the drunks and their drinking-related fights.

In 1910, Nevada passed an anti-gambling law so strict that it was illegal to even follow the western custom of flipping a coin for the price of a drink. Within weeks, however, underground gambling began to flourish.

On March 16, 1911, Las Vegas incorporated, covering an area of approximately twenty square miles. The city's population was about 800. At the same time, Clark County had 3,321 residents.

By 1930, the population of Las Vegas had reached 5,165. Shortly thereafter, three events occurred that permanently altered the face of Las Vegas, Clark County, and Nevada. As a side effect, they also led to the initiation of Las Vegas Valley as a cash cow for organized-crime families across the country.

First, on March 19, 1931, gambling was legalized in Nevada. A month later, six gaming licenses were issued in Las Vegas, the first going to Stocker's Northern Club on Fremont Street.

Second, state divorce laws were liberalized. With easier residency requirements, "quickie" divorces could be attained in only six weeks. Short-term residents flocked to Nevada. In Las Vegas, many of them stayed at dude ranches, the forerunners of the sprawling Strip hotels of today.

And third, construction began on Hoover Dam, generating a population boom and boosting the Valley's economy, which was in the grip of the Great Depression.

Small-town Las Vegas would soon be on its way to becoming the entertainment and gambling capital of the world.

But the influx of people and money would later earn Vegas another name: Sin City.

Benjamin Siegel

Ten years later, the first Strip casino appeared when the El Rancho Vegas opened on April 3, 1941. The Last Frontier followed on October 30, 1942. The next Strip property to arrive on the scene, in 1946, was the one that is acknowledged as the first of those backed substantially by mob money: Bugsy Siegel's Flamingo.

Benjamin Siegel was born in Brooklyn in 1905. While growing up he developed a reputation for having a vicious temper, which earned him the nickname of "Bugsy." As a teenager in New York, Siegel befriended Meyer Lansky and, with a group of other young tough guys, operated the Bug and Meyer Mob. Eventually, they teamed up with future New York City crime boss Charlie "Lucky" Luciano. In spite of alleged involvement in crimes ranging from bootlegging to murder, Siegel was able to avoid being convicted of any serious charges.

Bugsy had the looks of a Hollywood leading man and made frequent trips from New York to Los Angeles. He enjoyed the company of famous entertainers, many of whom liked the idea of socializing with the increasingly powerful gangster. His infatuation with Hollywood led him to move west to help establish the mob-controlled Trans-America wire service to compete with the Continental Press Service, which provided bookmakers with the results of horse races from across the country.

In pursuit of this objective, Siegel made an appearance in Las Vegas in 1942. His enterprise was legal in Nevada, where all potential clients held county licenses. He signed up a number of subscribers to the service, each paying a hefty fee.

It's estimated that Siegel's income from the Las Vegas bookies was about $25,000 per month. During this brief visit, Siegel came to appreciate the tremendous earning potential of the Las Vegas casinos.

In early 1946 Siegel saw an opportunity to establish himself in the Las Vegas gambling business. A Hollywood nightclub owner named Billy Wilkerson had attempted to build a casino in Vegas called the Flamingo. The effort faltered and the partially completed resort was sitting idle. Bugsy packed his clothes and money and headed back to Vegas to take over the Flamingo project. He was confident that if his personal finances weren't enough to finish the job, his hoodlum friends could be convinced to invest in his dream: building the first truly posh hotel and casino in the Las Vegas desert.

Bugsy hired the Del Webb Construction Company of Phoenix to complete the Flamingo. According to the book *The Green Felt Jungle*, the cost, initially estimated at $1.5 million, ballooned to $6 million. The many reasons cited for the huge cost overrun included Siegel's insistence that the Flamingo be built like a fortress, constructed of steel and concrete where less expensive materials would have sufficed. He also wanted the best in furnishings, importing wood and marble at exorbitant costs. Each guest room even had its own sewer line, adding $1 million to the bill.

So soon after the end of World War II, not all of the supplies Siegel ordered Webb to use were readily available; such circumstances proved to be only minor annoyances to Bugsy, who simply turned to the black market for his needs. He got whatever he wanted, but had to pay outrageous prices. To make matters worse, the illegal suppliers sometimes delivered a load of expensive merchandise during the day, then returned at night to steal it back. Finally, they showed up at the site the next morning to sell Siegel the same items all over again.

The black marketeers weren't deterred from their larcenous actions by Bugsy's fearsome reputation, and Las Vegas police officer Hiram Powell was equally unimpressed with the gangster. The bronco buster from Texas arrived in Vegas in 1941 to compete in a rodeo and never left. He was hired as a cop in 1942 and recalled his first encounter with Siegel in a 2002 interview.

"It was a winter morning in the mid-1940s. I pulled Siegel over for a traffic violation at East Charleston and Fifth Street [now Las Vegas Boulevard]. When he handed me his license, there was a hundred dollar bill folded up with it. That was a lot of money at the time, but I let the bill drop to the ground. The last I saw of it, it was blowing down Charleston. I gave Siegel his ticket and let him go. Back then he had a reputation as a tough guy, but as far as I was concerned he was just another punk."

Bugsy may have been just another thug to Powell, but the cop soon learned he was a well-connected one.

"About an hour after I stopped Siegel, I got a radio message to return to the station. The chief asked me what had happened between Siegel and me. I told him the story and then he fired me," Powell recalled. The officer was reinstated a day later, but Siegel was never one of his favorite people.

Bugsy's political clout, however, wasn't able to help him when it came to his financial woes at the Flamingo. Quickly running out of his own estimated $1 million, he made numerous trips back to the Midwest and East Coast in search of additional funding. Over time, he was able to get his gangland associates to invest $3 million, but that still left him a couple million in the hole. Seeing the Flamingo project as a bottomless pit, Bugsy's hoodlum friends cut off their largesse. Some even began to wonder if Siegel was just an incompetent businessman or if something more sinister was behind the burgeoning cost of the Flamingo. Was it possible that Bugsy had sticky fingers and was stealing from his friends? Coming under that type of suspicion from his investment partners didn't bode well for the would-be gambling tycoon, neither financially nor physically.

In June of that year, an incident took place that convinced Siegel's New York pals that his ego was growing as fast as the Flamingo's debt. James Ragan, the owner of Continental Press Service, was gunned down in Chicago in an attempted hit. Surprisingly, the man survived the attack and was recovering in a hospital six weeks later when he suddenly died. An autopsy revealed that Ragan had enough mercury in his body to kill him twice over. In spite of an around-the-clock police guard, the Chicago Outfit had apparently found a way to spike the dead man's soft drinks with the poison. The Chicago people quickly took over Continental Press, eliminating the need for the mob-owned Trans-America. Still, Bugsy needed his income from the wire service and figured his colleagues liked the extra cash, too. He also needed more money for the Flamingo. He flew to New York to discuss the situation with the board of directors of the Combination.

In a stunning presentation, Siegel told some of the most dangerous men in America that if they wanted Trans-America to stay in business, they'd have to give him $2 million, which happened to be the amount he owed Del Webb. That was the deal, take it or leave it. With that he walked out, leaving a room full of gangsters looking at each other in open-mouthed amazement.

Back in Las Vegas, Siegel was like a man possessed in trying to get the Flamingo ready for opening. He ordered everyone on twelve-hour shifts and seven-day work weeks. With the Vegas valley's population at around a meager 40,000, additional craftsmen were flown in from Los Angeles, Denver, San Francisco, and Salt Lake City to supplement the local labor pool. Construction continued to be plagued by design flaws and poor workmanship.

Trouble was also brewing in Los Angeles, where the bookies were looking for relief from being forced to pay fees to both Chicago's Continental Press Service and the still-operating Trans-America. They didn't like it, but knew it was dangerous to cease doing business with either one. Siegel told them to go to hell. As the dissatisfaction grew, his attitude placed the local people running Trans-America in an increasingly tough spot.

Though unfinished, the Flamingo opened on December 26, 1946. The casino, lounge, theater, and restaurant were ready to go, and that was enough for Bugsy. Dressed in a white tie and swallowtail coat, his Beverly Hills girlfriend Virginia Hill by his side, the handsome gangster was ready for his big night. Unfortunately, it proved to be a disaster, a flop that was not well-received back east.

The day started out bad when planes Siegel had hired to bring in specially invited guests from Los Angeles were grounded due to poor flying weather in California. Even so, some entertainers and celebrities did make it to the Flamingo that night. They included Jimmy Durante, performing the leadoff act, followed later by the Xavier Cugat Band. Actors George Sanders and George Raft also appeared.

Siegel's run of bad luck continued in the casino: It lost money. As word of the losses made their way to Bugsy during the evening, he became irate. He reportedly took his anger out on some of the guests, becoming verbally abusive and throwing out at least one family.

Two weeks later, as the losing streak continued, Bugsy closed the Flamingo's doors. He decided to wait for the hotel to be finished to reopen, hopefully with better results.

As Siegel cooled his heels waiting for his next chance at gambling stardom, he received disturbing news from New York. Lucky Luciano, who had been exiled to Italy as part of a deal he made with the government to get out of prison after a racketeering conviction, had convened a meeting of the Combination in Havana and Bugsy wasn't on the list of invitees. In Siegel's world, a snub like that often boded ill for the one being excluded.

Sensing that he might be in trouble, Bugsy flew to Havana on his own to see Luciano. Meeting in the headman's hotel suite, the talk eventually turned to the Flamingo. Siegel sang its praises, but Lucky was unimpressed with his underling's descriptive phrases of glitz and glamour. He was more interested in where his partner's $3 million investment stood. Siegel pleaded for more time, a year, to get the Flamingo open again and turn it into the revenue producer he was sure it could be.

Luciano dismissed Siegel with the admonishment that he should go back to Vegas and behave himself. The boss also ordered him to give up the wire service and let the Chicago Mob have the operation to itself. With that, the famous Siegel temper kicked into high gear. In no uncertain terms, Bugsy told Lucky what he could do with his orders, then stormed out of the meeting.

Few if any men talked to Lucky Luciano the way Siegel had and lived very long to tell about it. Bugsy would be no exception.

The Flamingo reopened on March 27, 1947. For the first three weeks it continued to operate in the red, and then things began to turn around. In May it was $300,000 in the black. Bugsy had been apprehensive after his return from Havana, but the positive financial reports calmed him down. His vision was finally being realized. The Flamingo was on its way to becoming the gold mine he'd predicted. He was sure Lucky and the others would be pleased they had listened to him. However, the Flamingo's success was a case of too little, too late for Siegel.

On the night of June 20, a now-confident Siegel was relaxing in the living room of Virginia Hill's mansion in Beverly Hills. Conveniently for her, she was away on vacation in Paris, but his trusted friend Al Smiley was with him. Suddenly, rifle shots rang out from outside the living-room window. Two slugs struck Siegel in the face. One of them ejected his left eye, which was found on the floor some 15 feet away from his body. Benjamin Siegel had been murdered at the age of 41. Bugsy was dead, but Las Vegas was just coming to life.

Morris Dalitz

Not long after Bugsy's permanent departure from the Las Vegas scene, another key player arrived in town.

Morris "Moe" Dalitz was born in Boston in 1899. His father, Barney, operated a laundry and taught Moe the business as he was growing up. The family moved to Michigan where Barney opened Varsity Laundry in Ann Arbor, catering to University of Michigan students.

As time went by, Moe opened a string of his own laundries in Michigan before branching out to Cleveland in the 1930s. Once there, he expanded his earning potential by getting involved in the bootlegging business and becoming associated with the Mayfield Road Gang. By the time prohibition ended, Dalitz had opened several illegal gambling joints. His two careers—legitimate business owner and criminal bootlegger and casino operator—would combine to lead him to Las Vegas.

In the first instance, Moe's laundry business resulted in his developing a close relationship with a very important man: Jimmy Hoffa. This happened in 1949, when the Detroit Teamsters local demanded a five-day work week for laundry drivers. Laundry owners, including Dalitz, strongly opposed the union's position. Negotiations reached an impasse, with each side unwilling to budge.

Dalitz, the shrewd businessman, saw a way around the issue. He had the owner representatives bypass the local's negotiator, Isaac Litwak, and reach out directly to its former business agent and current leader of the Detroit Teamsters, Jimmy

Hoffa. Agents of the laundry owners asked what it would take for Hoffa to intervene on behalf of the owners. Hoffa's man said $25,000 would do the trick. The owners agreed. Neither side bothered to inform Litwak of the developments.

During a subsequent bargaining session, Litwak was confident he had the owners on the ropes. Late in that meeting the door opened and in walked Jimmy Hoffa. He told the group there would be no strike and he wanted the contract signed on the owners' terms, with no five-day work-week provision. The stunned Litwak had no choice but to comply.

In the great scheme of things, this transaction wasn't a particularly big deal. But it did open the door for something much bigger ten years later: multi-million-dollar loans from the Teamster Pension Fund to finance the mob-controlled casinos of Las Vegas.

Also in 1949, Moe Dalitz found a business opportunity in Vegas similar to Bugsy Siegel's Flamingo experience. Another Strip hotel and casino construction project had been abandoned and was available to anyone who could come up with the right money. Dalitz, casino-savvy from running his own illegal businesses, and three of his cronies from Cleveland raised the funds and purchased the Desert Inn. The Strip's fourth resort opened on April 24, 1950.

The 1950s saw seven more casinos added to the Strip, all allegedly backed by mob money from the Midwest and East Coast. The Sands and Sahara opened in 1952, the Riviera and Dunes in 1955, the Hacienda in 1956, the Tropicana in 1957, and the Stardust in 1958. One existing property changed names when the Last Frontier became the New Frontier in 1955. During that same time period the population of the Valley grew from 45,000 to 124,000.

The '50s also saw an increase in the number of celebrity weddings held in Las Vegas. Among the more notable, Rita Hayworth and Dick Haymes were wed in 1953, Kirk Douglas and Ann Buydens in 1954, Joan Crawford and Alfred Steele in 1955, Carol Channing and Charles Lowe in 1956, Steve Lawrence and Eydie Gorme in 1957, and Paul Newman and Joanne Woodward, and David Janssen and Ellie Graham exchanged vows in 1958.

Moe Dalitz and Jimmy Hoffa combined to bring the first installment of Teamster Pension Fund money into Las Vegas in 1959. But the $1 million loan didn't help to build a hotel and casino. It financed the Dalitz-controlled Sunrise Hospital.

To help assure that the new medical facility would have some business, Hoffa worked out a deal between his union members, their employers, and Sunrise for the provision of medical treatment. The employers agreed to pay $6.50 per month for each union employee into a fund that paid the provider of the medical services, Sunrise Hospital. In turn, the hospital promised to set five beds aside specifically for union members and provide basic medical care.

After this successful beginning, more Teamster money found its way to Vegas in the 1960s and beyond. The millions of dollars in loans were used to build or expand casinos, shopping malls, and golf courses. This was at a time when most lending institutions wanted nothing to do with entrepreneurs from notorious Sin City.

In 1966, the Aladdin and Caesars Palace joined the growing number of Strip resorts. The Teamster-financed Circus Circus opened in 1968.

More big-name celebrity weddings took place in Vegas in the '60s. Mary Tyler Moore and Grant Tinker were married at the Dunes in 1962 and Betty White and Allen Ludden said their vows at the Sands in 1963. The Dunes hosted its second big marriage of the decade when Jane Fonda and Roger Vadim tied the knot in 1965. The next year, Xavier Cugat and Charo were hitched at Caesars Palace. Two mega-nuptials occurred in 1967, between Elvis Presley and Priscilla Beaulieu at the Aladdin, and Ann Margret and Roger Smith at the Riviera. Wayne Newton and Elaine Okamura were wed at the Flamingo in

1968. By the end of the decade, the valley's population had reached 273,000, more than doubling in ten years.

As the years passed, Moe Dalitz continued to use his friendship with Jimmy Hoffa to facilitate loans sought by Las Vegas businesses. In spite of his power, Dalitz kept a low profile, remaining an intensely private man. He became heavily involved in charity work and in 1976 was named Humanitarian of the Year by the American Cancer Research Center and Hospital. In 1982 he received the Torch of Liberty Award by the Anti-Defamation League. Moe Dalitz died in 1989 of natural causes.

As the '60s came to a close, Las Vegas was booming. It was an "open town" for organized-crime families nationwide, many of which had already established their presence. But one of them held a position of dominance—Chicago.

2

Chicago

The history of organized crime in Chicago is rife with the names of some of the most infamous gangsters ever to make a dishonest dollar in this country. They include the likes of "Big Jim" Colosimo, Johnny Torrio, Sam Giancana, Frank Nitti, and the legendary Al Capone.

For our purposes, we're going to focus on two lesser-known men, men who were young up-and-comers in the Chicago Mob during the days of Capone. These were guys who rose to power in the '50s and remained there through much of the '80s. They were in the hierarchy when a young enforcer named Tony Spilotro became a made man in the Outfit. And during the fifteen years Tony was in Las Vegas, they were his superiors.

Tony Accardo

Anthony "Joe Batters" Accardo was born in Chicago's Little Sicily on April 28, 1906. At the age of five he enrolled in grade school, but by the time Accardo was 14 he'd become disenchanted with the education system. So had his parents, who, like many others of that era, filed a delayed birth-record affidavit, stating that their son had actually been born in 1904. The additional two years allowed Tony to drop out of school and begin working.

Accardo had several minor brushes with the law in his youth—among them a 1922 arrest for a motor-vehicle violation and a 1923 charge in conjunction with an incident at a pool hall where organized-crime figures were known to hang out—but he never spent a single night in jail. Around this time the teenage Accardo joined the Circus Café Gang, named for its headquarters, the Circus Café on North Avenue. Among his fellow gang members was James Vincenzo De Mora, also known as Vincent Gibardi. De Mora later made his mark as Machine Gun Jack McGurn. Under that name he became one of Al Capone's most trusted hit men and was the reputed planner of the 1929 St. Valentine's Day Massacre.

By 1926, the Capone organization was expanding rapidly and Big Al needed more soldiers for his army. McGurn, having experienced Accardo's criminal abilities first hand as a member of the Circus Café Gang, recommended his friend to Capone as a possible recruit. Tony had already participated in nearly every racket and was a prime candidate for advancement. So it was that Accardo graduated from the street gangs of Chicago to Scarface Al's powerful Outfit. He was brought before Capone at the Metropole Hotel on Michigan Avenue and, grasping the hand of his sponsor, Machine Gun Jack, swore the oath of Omerta. Having taken the mob's vow of silence, the 20-year-old Accardo became a made man in the Chicago Outfit.

Tony was one of Capone's bodyguards on September 20, 1926, when eleven cars occupied by members of Bugs Moran's rival North Side Gang attacked Capone's Cicero headquarters, the Hawthorne Inn. Thousands of machine-gun rounds poured into the building. As soon as the bullets started to fly, Accardo pulled Al to the floor and lay on top of him to shield his boss from the onslaught. At the conclusion of the assault a couple of bystanders and several minor gangsters had been wounded, but miraculously, no one was killed.

Tony's actions that day earned him a position as one of Capone's regular protectors, and he soon began taking on more important assignments for the Outfit. He allegedly earned his nickname by smashing the skulls of two men with a baseball bat; when Jack McGurn told Capone about the beating, the boss was impressed and said, "This boy is a real Joe Batters." The name stuck, and from that point on Tony was known as Joe Batters to his criminal colleagues.

Accardo also worked closely with Capone's other top assassins: McGurn, Albert Anselmi, and John Scalise. It's believed the four went to New York City in 1928 to kill Capone's friend-turned-enemy, Frankie Yale, who was gunned down in Brooklyn. It marked the first time a Thompson submachine gun was used in a gang-related hit in the Big Apple.

Accardo continued to do the heavy work into the '30s. When the Chicago Crime Commission released its first "Public Enemies" list in 1931, Tony came in at number seven.

After Capone went to prison in 1931 for income-tax evasion, Joe Batters moved on to do the bidding of Al's successor, Frank Nitti. In 1933, the new boss appointed Accardo as capo (captain) of a street crew, in command of a dozen or so soldiers. The promotion made Tony one of the top twelve members of the Chicago Mob.

In the early 1940s, Accardo's career took another giant step forward when many of his superiors were implicated in what was known as the Hollywood Extortion Case. As the men above them went to jail, Tony and others moved up the ladder. Eventually, two gangsters were in contention for the top spot: Tony Accardo and Dago Lawrence Mangano. Before the issue could be settled by a vote, the unfortunate Mangano was murdered. Unidentified assailants in a passing car fired shotguns and .45 pistols at him, riddling his body with more than 200 shotgun pellets and five 45-caliber bullets. With his competition gone, Arccado became the number-one man in the Chicago Outfit in 1945.

In 1946, Accardo's people approached James Ragan, the owner of the Continental Press wire service that provided racing results to bookies, and offered to buy him out. It was an offer Ragan felt he could refuse, and he turned them down. To people with Accardo's mindset, that was bad enough. But Ragan compounded his sin by bringing the Outfit's proposal to the attention of law enforcement. Shortly thereafter, he was eliminated; his body had barely cooled to room temperature before the Outfit had control of Continental Press.

In 1950, a federal crime commission officially recognized Accardo as the boss of Chicago's crime syndicate. However, his reign was cut short in 1957 when an IRS investigation forced him to step down and turn control of the Outfit over to Sam Giancana. At Giancana's request, Tony agreed to stay on in an advisory capacity. Most law enforcement personnel believe that Accardo was actually the brains behind the Outfit for the next several years, keeping a low profile behind a series of "bosses." One such figurehead was another career criminal, Joseph Aiuppa, who ascended to the throne of the Chicago mob in 1971.

Joe Aiuppa

Joseph John Aiuppa was born on December 1, 1907, in Melrose Park, Illinois. According to a 1958 FBI report, an examination of Aiuppa's Selective Service questionnaire submitted in 1940 showed that he attended school only until the third grade. Aiuppa's record from the federal penitentiary in Terra Haute, Indiana, from which he was released on March 3, 1958, after serving a year and a day for an unspecified offense, stated that he left school in 1918, at 11 years of age.

After working for the Alming Greenhouse in 1922 and as

a driver for the Midwest Cartage Company in 1925, Aiuppa purchased the Turf Lounge in Cicero, Illinois, in 1930. That same year he also became a partner in the Taylor Company, which manufactured gambling equipment.

The same FBI report indicates that Aiuppa was connected with the John Dillinger and Alvin Karpis gangs in the early 1930s. In 1935, he joined the Capone Outfit, then being run by Frank Nitti, as a muscleman and gunner. He went on to take control of the Outfit's criminal activities in Cicero and the western suburbs of Chicago. In 1958, Aiuppa was recognized as the boss of the "strip," a row of illegal gambling and strip joints located in Cicero.

In the mid-1950s, when the Senate's McClellan Committee investigated organized-crime's infiltration of labor unions, Joe Aiuppa was summoned. When he appeared to testify, the gangster exercised his Fifth Amendment rights 56 times.

The FBI document concludes with this warning:

SUBJECT IS KNOWN TO CARRY GUNS AND HAS ALLEGEDLY COMMITTED MURDER IN THE PAST AND SHOULD BE CONSID-ERED ARMED AND DANGEROUS.

In 1962, Joe Aiuppa earned the moniker "Doves" when he was arrested upon returning from a hunting trip in Kansas. Some 500 dead birds, all doves, were found in his possession, far exceeding the 24-bird limit.

Although Doves was vicious and loyal, he wasn't considered especially bright or articulate. He rose through the ranks to become one of the top three men in the Outfit, but didn't advance further for several years. His opportunity to move to the top came in 1971, when the current boss, Felix "Milwaukee Phil" Alderisio, was convicted of bank fraud. Backed by Tony Accardo, Joe Aiuppa was picked to fill the resulting vacancy.

So, in 1971, the two most powerful men in the Chicago

Outfit were Joe Aiuppa and the behind-the-scenes "real boss," Tony Accardo. Between them, the pair had only about 12 years of formal education, but nearly 90 years of criminal experience.

3

Lefty and Tony

Two of the key figures on the Las Vegas scene during the mob's heyday were Frank "Lefty" Rosenthal and Tony "the Ant" Spilotro. They were both born in Chicago and grew up in the same neighborhoods, where they met and became friends. Each became involved with the Chicago Outfit in a different capacity. Rosenthal, because he was Jewish and ineligible to become a made man, was connected simply as an "associate." Spilotro was a full-fledged member of the organized-crime family. Nevertheless, both men became highly adept in their respective areas of expertise. Following is a brief look at their lives through 1971, when Spilotro imposed himself upon Rosenthal's relatively peaceful life in Las Vegas.

Frank Rosenthal

Frank "Lefty" Rosenthal was born in Chicago in 1929, the son of a produce wholesaler. However, his father's business didn't appeal to young Frank, who, as he grew up, became more interested in what was going on at racetracks and ballparks than in the price of oranges. His innate talent for sports wagering caught the attention of professionals and at the age of 19, Frank was offered a job as a clerk with Bill Kaplan of the Angel-Kaplan Sports Service in Chicago.

Lefty developed his oddsmaking skills with the help of Kaplan and some illegal bookmakers, and he did so quickly. He was a natural when it came to formulating betting lines on sporting events. As the years passed, Rosenthal gained a reputation as one of the premier handicappers in the country, and was a top earner for the Outfit's illegal gambling operations. Lefty was on top of his game, but fame and fortune had their price.

In 1960, Rosenthal's name appeared on a series of lists of known gamblers produced by the Chicago Crime Commission and he decided it was time to get out of town. The following year Frank moved to Miami, hoping to keep a lower profile.

But his reputation and known affiliation with organized-crime had preceded him to Florida. It wasn't long before the numbers guru came to the attention of the Senate's McClellan Committee on gambling and organized crime.

In 1961, Attorney General Robert Kennedy asked the Permanent Subcommittee on Investigations to look into illegal gambling activities. Lefty was called to testify before Senator McClellan's committee. During his appearance, the bookmaker was less than candid, invoking the Fifth Amendment 37 times. A few months later, Rosenthal was among a large number of bookies and players arrested as part of an FBI crackdown on illegal gambling. The Miami police then got in on the act and were soon arresting the 32-year-old on a regular basis. The same cops who had initially turned a blind eye to his bookmaking activities were now putting on some big-time heat.

Things got worse for Rosenthal in 1962 when he was indicted for attempting to bribe a college basketball player.

Although he maintained his innocence, he eventually pled no contest to the charges.

Despite his altercations with the law, Lefty persevered, and was still in Miami when his old buddy, Tony Spilotro, arrived in 1964. However, the FBI was keeping an eye on Rosenthal and the presence of Spilotro, a suspect in multiple murders in Chicago, only increased the gambler's unwanted visibility and made his public life more difficult.

By 1966, Lefty had had his fill of Miami and decided to move to a location where people in his line of work were treated with a little more respect. He settled on the booming gaming city in the desert, Las Vegas. Not long after his arrival in 1967, he bought into the Rose Bowl Sports Book, later relocating to the Strip and the mob-controlled Stardust. Lefty was moving up fast and his future looked bright. But in 1968, something happened that had a major impact on his life, and eventually the lives of several others. He fell in love.

Geri McGee moved from California to Las Vegas in the late 1950s. An attractive woman, she worked as a topless show-girl at the Tropicana and Dunes and as a cocktail waitress and hustler around the casinos. When Lefty met her it was love at first sight, at least on his part. He was in a hurry to tie the knot, but Geri had reservations about settling down. Her concerns faded when Lefty placed a hefty stash of cash and jewelry in a safe deposit box for her to keep if the marriage didn't work out. The two were wed the following year.

Initially, everything went well for the newlyweds. Geri liked to spend money and her husband made plenty of it. But in 1970, Lefty was indicted again for bookmaking. This was the kind of thing that could jeopardize his eligibility to be licensed as a casino manager. His links to organized-crime figures posed a similar threat, since the Nevada Gaming Control Board was likely to deny licensing upon learning of such relationships. Consequently, in 1971, as Lefty ascended to a manager's position at the Stardust and struggled to keep his nose clean, it came as an unwelcome shock when his life-long pal, the increasingly notorious Chicago gangster Tony Spilotro, moved to town.

Anthony Spilotro

Tony Spilotro was born in Chicago on May 19, 1938. He was the fourth of six sons born to Italian immigrants Patsy and Antoinette Spilotro. Patsy opened Patsy's Restaurant at the corner of Grand and Ogden avenues. Although the eatery became a hangout for members of the Outfit, there's no evidence that Patsy had any involvement in criminal activity.

Like Lefty Rosenthal, young Spilotro shunned involvement in his father's business. The street interested him more than spaghetti. In school, he developed a reputation as a tough kid, bullying and intimidating classmates and teachers alike. Several of his fellow students said he exhibited the "little-man's syndrome." Some speculate that his diminutive size, around five-feet-five, may have earned him the nickname "the Ant." Others say it was simply short for Anthony. Nancy Spilotro, Tony's wife, isn't sure where the name came from, and thinks it was a creation of the press. Another relative believes it's a derivative of "pissant," an epithet assigned to Tony by a Chicago cop. In any case, it was a handle Spilotro didn't like.

By 1955, his father had passed away and Tony was thrown out of school for continued misconduct. Now on the streets full-time, Spilotro took up with other kids in the same situation. He was soon the scourge of the neighborhoods, stealing cars, robbing stores, and developing a reputation for viciousness. When Tony was 18, his actions caught the attention of Sam "Mad Sam" DeStefano.

DeStefano was connected to the Outfit and operated a loan-sharking business. He was known to friend and foe as being completely insane. When he dealt with his enemies, his depravity knew no bounds. Mad Sam preferred to use an ice pick on his victims, but wasn't above slicing, shooting, or incinerating them, depending on his mood. Although he was unstable, the bosses kept him around; he was a good earner. In addition to being an accomplished torturer and killer, Sam had another talent. He could spot street kids who demonstrated the same capacity for brutality that he had. DeStefano liked what he saw in Tony Spilotro and recruited him as an enforcer; Spilotro accepted.

On January 15, 1961, Tony took a break from his normal activities to marry Nancy Stuart. Born in Milwaukee in 1938, she was living in Chicago when they met. According to John L. Smith's book *Of Rats and Men*, while the Spilotros were on their honeymoon in Belgium, Tony was thrown out of the country for possession of burglary tools.

Back in Chicago, Tony continued to work as one of Sam's heavies until 1962, when he got his big break. On May 15, two minor hoodlums, Billy McCarthy and Jimmy Miraglia, committed a fatal offense. They killed a couple of Outfit-connected guys—the Scalvo brothers—without permission, and they did it in a mob-inhabited residential area that the bosses had declared off-limits for murders. The powers-that-be wanted the culprits found and taken care of. The man who accomplished that task was bound to achieve an elevated status within the Outfit. Allegedly, Mad Sam suggested that Tony take a stab at it.

Opportunity had knocked and Tony wasn't shy about opening the door. In short order, he and his associates picked up McCarthy, but they still needed the name and location of the other condemned man. Their prisoner declined to cooperate, despite a severe beating. Surely, they thought, an ice pick to the scrotum would loosen the stubborn man's tongue, but it didn't. Getting frustrated, Tony decided it was time to quit playing nice and really apply some pressure. For McCarthy, it proved to be an eye-opening experience.

Putting McCarthy's head in a vise, Tony resumed the

questioning. Unfortunately for his victim, Spilotro didn't allow Fifth Amendment privileges during his interrogation sessions. Each time McCarthy refused to respond, Tony turned the handle on the vise, compressing McCarthy's skull. He finally obtained a breakthrough when one of McCarthy's eyeballs popped out. This was too much for the tough and loyal McCarthy to bear; he gave up Miraglia. The bodies of both men were later found in the trunk of an abandoned car in what became known as the M&M Murders. After this successful debut, Tony became a made man in the Outfit.

In 1963, Mad Sam got into a dispute with Leo Foreman, a real estate broker and one of his collectors. Not long after, Spilotro and an associate named Chuck Grimaldi reportedly lured Foreman to the home of Mario DeStefano, Sam's brother, in Cicero. The two beat Foreman, then dragged him into the cellar, where Mad Sam was waiting. Skipping an exchange of pleasantries, Sam got right down to business. He took a hammer to Foreman's knees, head, groin, and ribs. Next came twenty ice-pick thrusts, followed by a bullet to the head. The realtor's battered body was later found in the trunk of an abandoned car.

In 1964, with the heat mounting over the growing number of unsolved homicides in Chicago, the Spilotros spent some time in Miami. They had many friends and acquaintances there, including Frank Rosenthal. In 1966, they adopted their only child, an infant son, Vincent.

As the 1960s came to an end and the '70s began, the Chicago bosses initiated a cash-skimming operation involving the Las Vegas casinos under their control. They covered themselves by installing a front man as the gambling establishments' owner and appointing Lefty Rosenthal to manage the properties and keep an eye on things. This ensured that the casino count rooms could be accessed and cash removed before ever being recorded as revenue.

Having businessmen in place was great in theory, but there

was a lot of money involved and Las Vegas was growing by leaps and bounds. What if someone tried to skim the skim or otherwise rocked the boat?

To protect its interests from such problems, the Outfit needed someone on the scene with special talents, someone whose reputation served to discourage anyone from pilfering or causing other difficulties. And if intimidation wasn't enough, it had to be someone who wouldn't hesitate to take any action necessary to resolve the situation.

There was no need to recruit for the position; one of the Outfit's current members fit the criteria perfectly. Tony Spilotro was on his way to Sin City.

4

Mob-Run Las Vegas

The year was 1971. Don McLean's *American Pie* and Ike and Tina Turner's *Proud Mary* appeared on the pop music charts. After ten years there, American soldiers were still fighting and dying in Vietnam.

In Clark County, Nevada, the population had reached 275,000. Local law enforcement in the city of Las Vegas and unincorporated Clark County was the responsibility of two separate agencies. The Las Vegas Police Department handled the city. Everything else, including the Strip, came under the jurisdiction of the Clark County Sheriff's Department.

The gambling and tourism industries were flourishing. In the gaming arena, a milestone occurred when the Silver Slipper on the Strip and the Union Plaza downtown became the first casinos to hire female card dealers. Top entertainers appeared in casino showrooms and lounges. More than seven million tourists spent some time, and a lot of money, in the desert oasis.

Just as the gambling and entertainment drew the tourists, the money attracted the criminal element. Organized-crime families across the country considered Vegas an open city. Each of them was welcome to set up business there and many did. The various mobs exercised hidden ownership and control over several of the major casinos, most of which had been built with financing from the Teamster Pension Fund. The dominant group, however, hailed from Chicago.

Las Vegas locals and long-time visitors often speculate on what it was like to work in the casino business during those days. The following stories provide a little background on the way business was conducted back then. They come from three former casino insiders, all of whom were in supervisory or managerial positions and rubbed elbows with the wiseguys on a regular basis. Each man relates how his particular employer dealt with specific situations. To protect their identities, they're referred to here as Mario, Mickey, and Sammy.

The Insult

This incident took place in the late '60s, in the Crown Room of the International Hotel (now the Las Vegas Hilton).

"It was about three in the morning and another guy and I stopped in the Crown Room with our dates for a drink," Mario began. "I'm not going to name the other guy. But he was a real heavyweight in the casino business and his first name had a strong military ring to it.

"Anyway, there was a band from San Francisco on stage. They were rising stars and were being billed as the next coming of the Beatles. I don't know if it was because of booze or drugs, but this one guy turned out to be a real jerk. He looked at our table and said over the mike to my buddy, 'What's a bald old man like you doing with a pretty girl like her?'

"We let the crack slide, but the idiot wouldn't drop it. After a couple more wisecracks, my friend got up and made a call on a house phone. The president of the International lived in a suite at the hotel. Within a couple of minutes he showed up wearing pajamas covered by an overcoat. He went right to the stage and ordered the band to pack up their equipment and get out. Not just out of the hotel, but out of Vegas.

"The next day my friend made a call to the musicians union and the band suddenly couldn't get any bookings. They folded not long after that. Several years later I met one of the band members when he was in town for an electronics convention. We talked for a while and he said there were no hard feelings. After the band learned who they'd been throwing insults at, they considered themselves lucky to have gotten out of Vegas in one piece. It could have been worse.

"That's the kind of clout people like my friend had at the time. They could get top-of-the-line entertainers into their joints by making a phone call, and they could end someone's career the same way."

Cheaters

Customers who were caught cheating the casinos met different fates, depending on whom they had plucked and for how much.

"At my place on the Strip, we didn't go for the rough stuff," Mickey said. "You might mess a guy up a little and he comes back later with a gun or goes to the cops or the Gaming Control Board. The main concern was recovering our money and making sure the cheater knew he wasn't welcome back. But the cheats didn't know that when they got hustled off to the back room. I'm sure a lot of them thought they'd never be seen again.

"Usually they'd offer to give it up [the money]," Mickey continued with a smile. "They weren't very wise-assed or resistant at that stage of the game. But sometimes we'd make them lose it back. I remember this one guy who'd taken us for ten grand. We told him he could resolve the matter by going to a roulette table and staying there until he lost every dime. It was made clear to him that we'd be watching. After he'd lost his winnings he was to get out and never come back, not even to use the restroom. The guy couldn't agree fast enough. He dropped the money he owed us, and a thousand of his own for good measure. We never saw him again."

Sammy's experience with cheaters at a downtown casino was slightly different. "If it was only nickel-and-dime stuff, we'd just toss them. But if they took us for anything substantial, they'd be in a cast or on crutches for a while."

None of the roughed-up cheaters ever returned looking for revenge either. "Before we turned them loose, they understood what would happen if we ever saw them around again."

Mario's Strip employer reacted to some cheaters in a similar manner: "We had a room we jokingly referred to as the torture chamber. Some of the cheats left there with broken limbs. But I think the bigger problem for us was the deadbeats.

"These weren't cheaters. They were honest gamblers who, due to stupidity or bad luck, lost all their money and had to ask for casino credit so they could play some more. The amounts differed with each individual, but a hundred thousand dollars or more wasn't unusual. We checked these people out before extending the credit, of course. We knew where they lived, their income, and all that before they were approved.

"Most of them paid the money back without a problem, but a few seemed to forget about what they owed as soon as they got on the plane for home. We'd wait for a while, and if we didn't hear from them they'd get a phone call from one of our executives. The tenor of the conversation would be cordial and go something like this: 'We really appreciated your business and hope you come back soon. The next time you're in town your meals, room, et cetera are on us. Oh, and by the way, to avoid any embarrassment, you really should take care of your marker.'

"That would do the job most of the time. If it didn't, someone would pay a personal visit. It wouldn't be pleasant for the deadbeat, but we invariably got our money back."

The Skim

All three sources admitted that cash—lots of it—was removed from the casino count rooms before it was ever counted. At first the skim involved only the take from the table games, but eventually slot machine revenues were subject to manipulation as well. After the machines were emptied, the bags containing the coins or tokens were brought in and weighed to determine how much value they held. The scales were adjusted to show a lower-than-accurate weight, allowing a percentage of the take to go unrecorded. Whether the source of the money was from the tables or machines, the bottom line was the same: It was as though the money never existed. Although this activity was common knowledge to many of the managers, they typically weren't directly involved in the process. And it wasn't wise to show an interest in who took the money or where it went.

Sammy believes that authorities suspected him of being a courier for the skim. He cited an incident from the mid-'70s, when he was employed by one of the casinos under investigation. "My family and I flew to Phoenix for my father-in-law's funeral. I had a rental car reserved and when I went to pick it up, the guy told me the FBI had been asking about me. They wanted to know how long I'd have the car and where I'd be staying. That kind of thing. I just went about my business and never heard anything more about it."

The Wiseguys

According to Mario, Mickey, and Sammy, the wiseguys who ran or hung around the casinos weren't all that imposing. On the contrary, Mario said: "As long as you didn't cross them, they were mostly pretty good guys. They tended to be generous and helped a lot of the regular employees who were having financial or personal problems."

Sammy witnessed less interaction between the wiseguys

and casino employees, but noted, "I never had any problem with them. In fact, I liked most of them. I did my job and they didn't bother me."

Mickey agreed. "As long as you did what you were supposed to do and didn't stick your nose where it didn't belong, you had nothing to worry about. But if your curiosity got the best of you and you got too inquisitive, well, that could get you in trouble."

Tru Hawkins

Tru Hawkins, a radio personality on Las Vegas radio station KDWN, provides a different perspective of Vegas at that time. Hawkins' family moved to Las Vegas from California in 1945, when Tru was two years old. He got his first entertainment-related job, monitoring the KLAS radio transmitters at night, in the early 1960s. Later in the decade, he landed an on-the-air spot with KORK radio. An adult music station, it featured songs by artists currently appearing in Vegas. In the mid-'70s, Tru became the first morning man at KDWN, which also played adult music. The station later converted to talk radio and Hawkins now hosts the popular "Tru Hawkins Show."

Tru has personal recollections of Las Vegas from throughout the years, as well as stories his father shared with him about his employment at the Riviera starting in the mid-1950s.

"My father was hired at the Riviera as a cashier. He had a reputation as someone who could keep his mouth shut and it wasn't long before he was promoted to be manager of the casino cage. The money was stored in locked boxes until it was transferred to the bank. It was the practice to place one of the boxes filled with hundred-dollar bills on a shelf next to the back door to the cage. Mysteriously, in a short time an empty box would replace the full one. Those employees who were aware of the switch knew better than to question what was going on. Too much curiosity could be hazardous to their careers, or even their health."

Based on Tru's own experiences and what his father told him, two different pictures of the mobsters emerge. "If they liked you, they could be kind, considerate, and generous. On the other hand, if you crossed them, they were capable of cutting out your liver without thinking twice about it. Most everybody who worked around those guys knew that's the way it was.

"When I'd bump into one of the heavies, they'd ask, 'How ya doin', kid? Ya need anything? Can I do anything for you?' There was this one wiseguy who was a suspect in multiple murders. He learned that the son of one of the employees at the casino he was affiliated with had a serious medical problem that couldn't be treated locally at the time. He arranged for the kid and the parents to be flown to the UCLA Medical Center and stay there until the boy was taken care of. He didn't even discuss it with the father ahead of time. He just told him that everything was arranged and to be on the plane. It didn't cost the parents a dime."

Tru's occupation also allowed him to meet with Lefty Rosenthal on occasion. "In the '70s, I was working at the radio station and moonlighting as an announcer at KTBT-TV. At the same time, Frank Rosenthal was doing a weekly variety show that was taped at the Stardust and broadcast from the TV station. I ran into Lefty around the station every so often. He was one of the most charming guys you'd ever want to meet. But I knew he wasn't anybody you'd want to get on the wrong side of."

Regarding Las Vegas itself back then, Tru remembers it as a great place to live. "It was growing and there was a lot of stuff going on, but it was still a small town in a way, too. There's no place else I'd have rather been."

Joe the Bartender

"Joe" arrived in Las Vegas in 1966 and worked as a bartender in several clubs and casinos through the 1980s. He has his own memories and opinions of that era.

"It was a great town then, small and almost crime-free. Everybody knew there were mob guys running things and you didn't cross them. I wasn't in the gaming part of the operations and had very little contact with the wiseguys. I made sure I kept it that way."

Joe remembers a particular incident illustrating how the casinos dealt with employees who had sticky fingers. "I was working at a Strip casino and when I came in for the graveyard shift one night, I saw one of the dealers being escorted into the dealers break room by some security types. The dealers on break left the room in a hurry. Shortly afterward, a terrible series of screams came from inside. It turned out that the dealer had been caught hiding chips in his tie. He'd apparently been stealing for quite a while and had to be taught a lesson. They broke every one of his fingers on both hands and then threw him out. They also put the word out on the guy to the other casinos so that he'd never be able to get another casino job. It wasn't pretty, but that's the way it was. It sure made the other employees think twice before they'd try to give themselves a pay raise."

During those days, many entertainers would stop in the casino lounges for a drink after a performance and mingle with the patrons. Joe got to meet several headliners, including Frank Sinatra, Dean Martin, and Elvis Presley. "Almost all of them were great guys and treated the hired help with respect. There were a few assholes, though. These were the arrogant types who looked down on anyone getting paid an hourly wage. Fortunately, they were in the minority."

According to Joe, in addition to being a nice guy, Frank Sinatra was also generous. He related what he called a story "well-known to be true."

"I think it was in the late '60s and Sinatra was appearing at Caesars Palace. It happened that the daughter of one of the cocktail waitresses had been severely burned in a fire. The waitress, a single mother, was trying to take care of the kid and hold down her job at the same time. Her situation was the talk of the casino workers. Sinatra heard about it and had the waitress sent to his suite. She was nervous, figuring he probably wanted a little hanky-panky. When she got to his room, he asked her how much she earned in a year, including tips. She told him and he had his assistant write her a check for that amount right on the spot. Sinatra told her to take a year off and tend to her daughter. Her job would be waiting for her. That's the way it was then. Even the stars cared about the little people."

This was the Las Vegas that Tony Spilotro came to in 1971. It was a booming action-packed town, with tourists pouring in by the plane and carload. Honest visitors and locals enjoyed the ample sunshine, ate well, did a little gambling, and watched some of the best entertainers on the planet perform, all at reasonable prices.

Those who weren't so honest, however, found other ways to occupy their time and made plenty of money doing it.

5

The Spilotro Era Begins

Soon after settling into town with his wife Nancy and son Vincent, Tony Spilotro made his debut as a businessman. His first venture was opening a jewelry and gift shop at the Circus Circus Hotel and Casino. Using his wife's maiden name in order to prevent drawing attention to himself, Tony did business as Anthony Stuart, Ltd. Concessions in major casinos were generally hard to come by, especially for people with known ties to organized crime. According to Nevada gaming regulations, any casino doing business with such people could lose its license. Nevertheless, Circus Circus owner Jay Sarno chose to ignore the rules and let the mob-connected Spilotro open his shop. The fact that Sarno had obtained around $20 million in Teamster loans may very well have influenced his decision.

However, using the Stuart name didn't shield Tony's presence from local FBI agents. Their Chicago counterparts had alerted them to the move the moment the Spilotros set out for Vegas. Still, even though Tony was a suspect in multiple murders in Chicago, agents anticipated that his role in Las Vegas would be merely that of a gofer for Rosenthal and his cronies.

This was based on the belief that the various crime families with interests in Las Vegas casinos wanted to make money. For them to do so, their operations would have to maintain a low profile. Therefore, agents assumed, Tony wouldn't do anything to make waves. They were wrong.

Loansharking

Right from the start, Tony had things on his mind other than cashiering in his own store. Las Vegas was a 24-hour town, growing larger by the day. Many of the residents and new arrivals took jobs in the hotels and casinos as maids, valets, cleaners, food servers, and dealers. Most were paid low wages and relied heavily on tips to supplement their income. Sometimes their money didn't quite stretch to the next paycheck. These circumstances created a golden opportunity for someone who had money to lend and the ability to make sure he got it back. It was an ideal situation for an experienced loanshark like Spilotro.

Unfortunately, someone was already running loansharking operations in Las Vegas. His name was Gaspare Anedetto Speciale, known as Jasper to his customers, the police, and the FBI. He came to Vegas by way of New York and was with New York City crime boss Joe Columbo when Columbo was murdered in 1971. Mobsters visiting Sin City routinely sought an audience with Jasper and reportedly went through the ritual of kissing him on both cheeks when they met.

In deference to Jasper's connections, Tony didn't immediately try to displace him. On the contrary, "Tony kissed Jasper's ass when he first came to town, just like everybody else," as stated by retired FBI agent Michael Simon in a 1983 *Los Angeles Times* article. All the while, though, Spilotro bided his time, taking a share of the loansharking business without stepping on Jasper's toes. His restraint was rewarded a few years later; when Jasper went to prison in 1976 on a federal racketeering conviction, Tony emerged as the undisputed king of Las Vegas loansharks. In this case, he accomplished his rise the way Chicago preferred, without bloodshed or publicity.

A Murder Indictment Goes Away

In August 1972, Tony's efforts to establish himself in Vegas were interrupted by an incident from his past in Chicago: He was indicted for the 1963 murder of Leo Foreman. News of the indictment reached the Clark County Sheriff's Department when Sgt. Charles Lee, a former Chicago cop now working in Las Vegas, received a call from a Chicago homicide detective he knew. The detective told Lee about the indictment and that two Chicago detectives were flying to Vegas that night to arrest Spilotro. They wanted a couple of local officers to go along as backup. No problem there. It was what came next that Lee found chilling.

The Chicago cop warned Lee to be careful about whom he shared the information with. According to snitches in the Windy City, someone in Lee's department was on the Outfit's payroll.

Sergeant Lee broke the news to his boss and they put a plan in place to uncover the alleged rogue cop after Spilotro's arrest. Tony was taken into custody without incident and booked into the jail. After he was processed and taken to his cell, a covert surveillance of the jail began.

It wasn't long before John DeMoss, a 32-year-old officer with the Organized Crime and Homicide Unit, signed into the jail with his niece. He explained that he wanted to give the girl a tour of the facility. Once inside, he stopped at Tony's cell and spoke with the inmate. Afterward, he contacted an attorney for Tony, delivered a message from Rosenthal to Spilotro, and began making arrangements for bail. When confronted with his suspicious activity by his superiors, DeMoss opted to resign rather than undergo disciplinary proceedings. He wasn't unemployed for long, though. Almost immediately he was hired as a supervisor at the Rosenthal-managed Stardust. The ex-cop was later named as a suspect in gangland killings in Nevada and California, but was never arrested.

Even without DeMoss' help, Tony did okay. He was released from jail on $10,000 bail and, starting in September, shuttled back and forth between Chicago and Las Vegas. The arrangement allowed him to participate in trial preparation while continuing to take care of his Vegas interests.

"Scared to Death"

But there was a major concern for Tony regarding the Foreman trial: Sam DeStefano, his co-defendant along with Sam's brother Mario, was planning to act as his own attorney. Even worse, Mad Sam had been diagnosed with terminal cancer. Rumor had it that he was contemplating making a deal with prosecutors to avoid dying in prison. There was no doubt that any such arrangement would require Sam to give up the Ant and Mario. Tony's lawyer tried to get the cases severed, but failed.

With the legal system uncooperative, Tony went a different route. He took his pleadings to Tony Accardo. Five weeks before the trial, a person or persons unknown fired two shotgun blasts into Mad Sam's chest. In June 1973, Tony was acquitted of the Foreman charges. He was off the hook in Chicago for the time being, but the trial and the circumstances surrounding it had served the undesirable purpose of bringing Tony into the law-enforcement spotlight.

A 1974 study by the *Los Angeles Times* found that in the three years Tony had been in Vegas, more gangland-style murders had been committed there than in the previous 25 years combined. A casino executive and his wife were gunned down in front of their home. Another casino executive was murdered in a parking lot. A prominent lawyer was blown up in his Cadillac. A loanshark victim went missing and another casino boss was beaten and crippled for life. It didn't matter whether or not Spilotro was responsible for the violence. People, including the cops, believed he was, and as his reputation for viciousness grew, so did his boldness.

"Everybody on the Strip is scared to death of the little bastard. He struts in and out of the joints like Little Caesar," the *Los Angeles Times* quotes one casino owner as saying at the time. The same piece also quotes a store owner who first met Spilotro when Tony stopped in to buy clothes for his son. "When he came in the store the first time, you almost wanted to pat him on the head, until you looked into his eyes." Tony's eyes, described as pale blue and reptilian, looked through people, not at them. Many who dealt with Tony, including law-enforcement personnel, agreed you could find death in those eyes.

Another Witness Dies

Spilotro's fast rise as a force to be reckoned with in Vegas was interrupted again in 1974, when he was indicted by a federal grand jury in Chicago. This time he was one of six defendants charged with defrauding the Central States Teamsters Pension Fund of $1.4 million. Among his co-defendants were Joseph "Joey the Clown" Lombardo, one of Tony's superiors in the Chicago Outfit, and Allen Dorfman, believed to be a catalyst in arranging financial transactions between the Teamsters and organized crime. Dorfman had been convicted in a Teamster kickback case a few years earlier.

The government's scenario was complex, involving several companies and thousands of bookkeeping records. It could be a difficult case to get across to a jury. But the feds had an ace up their sleeve. The operator of one of the companies used to siphon money from the pension fund was cooperating. Prosecutors believed that their key witness, 29-year-old Dan Seifert, a Chicago businessman, would be able to walk the jurors through the maze of transactions in a manner they would be able to understand. If the prosecution proved successful, Tony and his pals would be off the streets for a long time.

In September 1974, three months before the trial was scheduled to begin, Seifert, his wife, and their four-year-old son stopped by Seifert's plastics factory early on a Friday morning. Four armed men wearing ski masks materialized and chased Seifert through the plant. They caught and killed the young husband and father with a shotgun blast to the head.

Seifert's murder had a chilling effect on the other witnesses. When the trial began, they crumbled on the stand as Tony's eyes bored into them. Spilotro was soon dropped from the case. All five of the other defendants were subsequently acquitted. Being an important witness in any case against Tony Spilotro was turning out to be extremely hazardous.

Meanwhile, back in Vegas and California, three more people met suspicious and untimely demises. Many suspected the murders were either carried out at Tony's behest or by the mobster himself. Spilotro was even charged in one of the homicides.

William Klim

On June 23, 1973, William "Red" Klim, a Caesars Palace employee, was shot and killed gangland style in the parking lot of the Churchill Downs Race Book. There were multiple theories regarding scenarios as to the motive for Klim's murder. One held that the deceased was cooperating with authorities in an investigation of illegal bookmaking that targeted Lefty Rosenthal. Another suggested that the dead man had information pertaining to Spilotro's implication in a fraud against the Teamsters Pension Fund. Yet another designated Klim as a loanshark who refused to pay the Ant a tribute. All three theories involved Tony either directly or as Rosenthal's protector.

Although Spilotro was charged with Klim's murder the following year, the case against him fell apart when witnesses were unable or unwilling to positively identify the killer.

Marty Buccieri

Marty Buccieri was a pit boss at Caesars Palace and a distant relative of Chicago underboss Fiori "Fifi" Buccieri. He reportedly had connections to most of the Vegas crime figures worth knowing and had used those connections to facilitate the granting of a number of Teamster Pension Fund loans to Allen Glick, CEO of Argent (Allen R. Glick Enterprises), the Outfit-installed owner of the Stardust, Hacienda, Fremont, and Marina casinos. In the summer of 1975, law-enforcement sources learned that Buccieri had approached Glick and demanded a $30,000 finder's fee for his help in obtaining the loans. At one point he's said to have physically threatened Glick. The Argent boss then informed Lefty Rosenthal—the behind-the-scenes power of the operation—of the incident.

A few days later, Buccieri was found shot to death. The law immediately suspected that Tony Spilotro was involved. Others in the know disagreed, citing the use of a 25-caliber weapon, rather than the .22 that was supposedly a Spilotro trademark. Regardless of the identity of the perpetrator, though, it's logical to conclude that Glick was a dangerous man to argue with or threaten.

Tamara Rand

Tamara Rand was an erstwhile friend and business partner of Allen Glick. She invested heavily in his Vegas casinos and, in spite of having no gaming experience, had signed a contract as a consultant at the Hacienda for $100,000 per year. Rand believed that through investments she had purchased five percent of Glick's casinos, so when Glick denied such a deal, she filed suit against him for breach of contract and fraud. A court trial could have blown the lid off the mob's hidden interests in the Las Vegas casinos. Consequently, on November 9, 1975, just days after a bitter argument between her and Glick, Tamara Rand was murdered at her home in San Diego.

Unlike the gun that killed Buccieri, the murder weapon in Rand's case was a .22, the reputed weapon of choice of Spilotro and his associates. Although Tony was a prime suspect in the Rand killing, there was insufficient evidence to charge him with the murder. One report even circulated that Tony had a solid alibi for the day in question. According to that story, while Rand was being rubbed out in San Diego, Tony was in Las Vegas chatting with an FBI agent who, for unknown reasons, had flown in from Chicago for a visit.

But former law-enforcement officers familiar with the Rand case and the Spilotro investigations don't recall Tony being cleared because of any such visit. They consider the report to be "dubious," and maintain that Spilotro was never taken off the table as a suspect.

At any rate, Tony gradually faded from the headlines in the Rand murder. That wasn't the case for Allen Glick, however. The relationship that had existed between Glick and the victim created a firestorm of speculation and media interest. By Thanksgiving, Glick was forced to issue a statement. He not only denied any involvement in the Rand murder, but also proclaimed that Argent had no connection to organized crime. Many in Las Vegas and law-enforcement circles found the latter contention to be absurd. Spilotro even got back in on the act by stating through his lawyer that he had absolutely no connection to Argent. Those in a position to know also greeted this declaration with great skepticism.

Around the time of the Buccieri and Rand murders, additional information about Allen Glick's activities began to surface from an unexpected source.

Newport Beach

In the 1970s, Bob Gatewood was a sergeant working with the police department in Newport Beach, California. He was assigned to the Organized Crime Unit. One day in 1973, he received a phone call from a friend, a Marine he'd met while undergoing SWAT training at Camp Pendleton. They'd become close and socialized together with their families.

Gatewood's friend told him he'd retired from the Marine Corps and taken a new job as a bodyguard for Allen Glick, who had a residence in an exclusive area south of Newport Beach. The ex-Marine had come to the conclusion that his new employer had some very shady associates and was probably involved in something illegal. He felt morally obligated to do something about it, but wasn't sure exactly what.

Due to his work in intelligence, Gatewood was familiar with Glick and his reported ties to organized crime and the Teamsters Pension Fund. During the discussion, Glick's bodyguard revealed that his position required that he accompany Glick on trips and at social gatherings, as well as receive a copy of the guest list to every event hosted by his boss. The former Marine agreed to provide information regarding Glick's activities and acquaintances, but only to Gatewood.

After the phone call, Sgt. Gatewood entered the information into the database of the national Organized Crime Intelligence Unit. He was soon receiving calls from agencies across the country, including the Nevada Gaming Control Board and, later, Las Vegas law enforcement.

For the next two years, the informant fed information to Bob Gatewood, who in turn passed it on to Nevada authorities. During that time the bodyguard became increasingly concerned for his personal safety and that of his family. He had his home checked for bugs and wiretaps. Sergeant Gatewood advised his friend that he could terminate his cooperation whenever he felt the situation had become too dangerous, but the flow of information continued until the informant switched jobs. He has since passed away from natural causes.

Bob Gatewood was never told exactly how the information his friend provided was used, but he believes it was instrumental in facilitating the investigations into Glick's involvement with organized crime.

Other Endeavors

In addition to loansharking, Tony had other money-producing irons in the fire, burglary and fencing stolen property chief among them. Burglars working for Spilotro eventually earned the nickname the Hole in the Wall Gang (HITWG). This handle resulted from their method of gaining entry into commercial buildings by making a hole in the wall or roof. But the thieves didn't limit themselves to breaking into businesses; they stole from private residences and hotel rooms with equal zeal. Jewelry and cash were prime targets.

The size of the burglary crew fluctuated depending on the nature of the job. Some small capers might require only one or two men, while a major heist could need six or seven. In the latter case, extra help was sometimes imported from Chicago or elsewhere.

The proceeds from a job were split among Spilotro and the burglars. For a big haul, Tony was obliged to send some of the profit to his Chicago bosses. He also had to pay a certain amount of overhead. Valets, maids, desk clerks, and others who provided information regarding the value and activities of potential victims were compensated for passing on the information.

One of these scams was operated out of two locations, a major Strip property and a popular restaurant, and involved valet parkers. The valets identified affluent guests and struck up conversations to obtain additional information about the guest's plans. For locals, valets could usually find address information with the registration papers in the vehicle. In the case of visitors, the name of their hotel was extracted during seemingly idle chitchat. Then, indicating long and short-term parking areas, the valet inquired as to how long the guest would be leaving their car. If the answer reflected a lengthy stay, the valet turned over the car to a burglar who, armed with keys to the residence, could conduct a leisurely burglary, using the victim's own vehicle to transport the booty. For out-of-towners, a friendly desk clerk at their hotel was contacted for specific room information. If the target's plans didn't allow the time for an immediate theft, the information was filed away for possible future use.

So, depending on the size of the score and the number of ways the loot had to be split, an individual burglar might earn enough money from a job to be able to take a few weeks off and live it up. However, if through faulty intelligence or bad luck, the break-ins weren't profitable, the thieves might be forced to strike again quickly just to maintain a basic standard of living.

Well, maybe "forced" is too strong a word. As a retired detective familiar with Spilotro's burglars told me: "Those guys loved to steal. It was what they did. They could be sitting in a restaurant with ten grand in their pockets and they'd go across the street to a convenience store to steal a pack of gum. They wanted the big money, sure. But stealing, in and of itself, was a necessity for them. They were addicted to it."

As Tony's status grew, additional sources of income materialized, too. The Ant and his gang weren't the only street criminals in Las Vegas. Other crooks, not mob-connected, wanted to share in the bounty and there was more than enough to go around. But Tony was running his budding underworld empire like a business. Legitimate entrepreneurs are required to get business licenses and pay related fees; if they're caught operating without the necessary permissions, they're subject to sanctions. Enterprising criminals wanting to get, or stay, in business also had to follow a certain protocol. They needed to get Tony's blessing and pay him a share of their profits, known in gangland parlance as a "street tax."

And it wasn't wise to think you could simply ignore Tony and go about your business without his finding out about it. He knew everything that went on within the Las Vegas criminal element. No one did anything—from contract killings to burglaries, robberies, fencing stolen property, or loansharking—without his approval and without paying him a monetary tribute where appropriate. And the sanctions for violating Tony's procedures could be much more severe than those imposed by a governmental licensing agency.

Tony Spilotro was becoming ever more powerful, and his organization was growing.

The Dunes

By 1975, Tony's entourage had increased dramatically with the arrival of his brother John and an influx of bookies, loansharks, burglars, and other heavies from Chicago. He decided to switch his base of operations to the Dunes, another Strip hotel-casino financed with Teamster money. This time he didn't open a shop; he used the card room of the casino as his office. Tony carried around a wad of money so he could accommodate those in need of loans. When he wasn't conducting business, he enjoyed fleecing suckers at the poker table or trying his hand at sports betting.

Major Riddle and Morris Shenker owned the Dunes. Riddle was one of Spilotro's favorite victims in the poker games. Tony and a couple of his cronies engaged in a "three-pluck-one" scam, where Riddle or some other naïve gambler sometimes lost thousands of dollars at a sitting. The Ant also had things his way when it came to sports wagering. Betting through illegal bookies, Tony made his picks, but didn't tender any cash. If he won, he expected to be paid. If he lost, no money changed hands. The bookies had little choice but to take their lumps. As one retired FBI agent told me: "Who in the hell was going to refuse Tony's action, or try to collect from him?"

Tony's presence at the Dunes didn't escape the attention of the Gaming Control Board. Their first effort to address the problem was by privately notifying Riddle and Shenker. The owners talked things over with Tony and he agreed to make himself scarce. The very next night, brother John Spilotro showed up in the card room. Answering phone pages as John Adams, he conducted business in Tony's stead. In a few weeks, Tony himself returned and it was back to business as usual.

The following year, the gaming regulators made another, more formal, effort to get Spilotro out of the casino. Riddle and Shenker were summoned to testify at a private hearing as to why Tony was being allowed to operate out of their card room.

Appearing first, Riddle said that until recently he didn't even know who Spilotro was, much less that he had Mafia connections. He claimed to have known Spilotro only as Tony and had never heard his last name. After learning Spilotro's identity, he asked Tony if he was lending money and using the Dunes as an office. Spilotro admitted making loans, but said they were interest-free. Riddle accepted that explanation as the truth. He concluded that Spilotro was "simply a good-hearted person." Riddle added, "I wouldn't want to talk to anybody nicer than Tony."

Next up was Morris Shenker. Not some run-of-the-mill novice when it came to legal proceedings, Shenker was a highly successful criminal defense attorney. He represented many of the nation's top criminals before the Kefauver Committee in the 1950s and was Teamster President Jimmy Hoffa's chief defense lawyer in the '60s.

Like Riddle, Shenker claimed to have been ignorant of

Spilotro's identity until recently. Now that he'd been made aware of who Tony was and his criminal associations, he vowed to take immediate action to remove the undesirable gangster from the Dunes.

But Tony wasn't waiting around to be ousted. He'd already found greener pastures.

Moving On Up

The Las Vegas Country Club and Estates, an exclusive walled community located near the Strip with guard posts at the entrance, was considered the place to belong in Las Vegas. Founded by former Cleveland bootlegger Moe Dalitz, its members included bankers, lawyers, doctors, and casino bosses. Initially, Tony and his associates gained access to the club through the memberships of his friends, such as Lefty Rosenthal. Since only members could sign for food, drinks, and tennis and golf fees, this arrangement proved awkward. Tony decided the only thing to do was join the club himself. He tried, but the membership committee rejected his application in June 1976.

Spilotro was furious. He complained to Rosenthal and others, demanding reconsideration. Under pressure, the membership committee realized the error of its ways and admitted the Ant. He was soon holding court in the card room, conducting meetings in the dining room, and playing gin rummy with some of the town's leading citizens. His wife Nancy learned to play tennis and became a regular on the courts. Even with all this going for him, it wasn't long before Tony found an even better deal.

Gold Rush

To accommodate the growing inventory of loot from his thriving burglary ring, Tony decided to open another jewelry store called the Gold Rush in a two-story building located on West Sahara, just off the Strip. It had a front door that could be operated by a buzzer located behind the counter; a private security company regularly swept the building for electronic bugs and monitored the building's alarm system. The second floor housed communications equipment, including two radio transmitters and receivers and five scanners that monitored police and FBI activities. Gang members with binoculars were sometimes stationed on the roof or parked on the street looking for signs of law-enforcement surveillance operations.

Tony, his brother John, and Herbert "Fat Herbie" Blitz-stein, a 300-pound convicted bookie from Chicago, operated the store itself. A loaded 9mm semi-automatic pistol and a .45 revolver were kept behind the counter, should anyone be foolish enough to try to rob the robbers.

Tony's store was staffed and equipped to make it difficult, if not impossible, to be breached by the law or other potential adversaries. But like any good businessman, Spilotro didn't place all his eggs in one basket. He took other precautions.

Intelligence

For centuries, countries have sought to spy on one another through the use of covert actions and, more recently, advancements in technology. When at war, it's critical for a nation's civilian and military leaders to know what their enemies are doing. With the right information, they can initiate defensive actions and countermeasures to prevent an enemy from successfully carrying out his plans.

Even in times of peace, intelligence-gathering activities are a critical piece of the foreign-policy puzzle. The main targets of these efforts are potential adversaries, but cases of friends caught spying on friends aren't unusual. Spies can be homegrown agents assigned to infiltrate targets or recruited from people already occupying sensitive positions within the opposition government. Over the years, money, blackmail, and sex have proved to be effective recruitment tools.

Intelligence-gathering efforts aren't limited to the international arena, however. Domestically, business competitors often engage in similar activities. And for years, the law has used undercover operations and informants in their investigations of crime. Being resourceful foes, the criminals also attempt to gain inside information about the law's plans and strategies. Additionally, they sometimes manipulate the legal system by corrupting lawyers, judges, jurors, and witnesses, usually via financial payoffs. When an offer of money doesn't do the trick, intimidation and violence, including murder, can be used to achieve the desired results.

The importance of good intelligence wasn't lost on Tony Spilotro. He and the other organized-crime families operating in Las Vegas took steps to keep up to speed on the law's movements.

Rogues, Bugs, Taps, and Raids

In the mid-1970s, Joe Blasko was a detective and Phil Leone a sergeant in the police department's anti-crime unit; they reported directly to Sheriff Ralph Lamb. On the side, they also provided information to Spilotro and other Las Vegas mobsters.

Blasko had been in trouble previously. In 1966, he and his partner were charged with murder, regarding the death of a cab driver they arrested. A coroner's inquest determined the man's death was the result of the use of excessive force by the arresting officers. The charges were later dismissed when a judge ruled the evidence was insufficient to warrant prosecution.

By March 1978, the FBI had developed sufficient probable cause to obtain warrants authorizing them to monitor the activities of Spilotro and other mobsters through the use of wiretaps and electronic eavesdropping. In addition, the feds had managed to infiltrate the Spilotro operation via an under-cover agent. Posing as a diamond fence named Rick Calise, agent Rick Baken was busy getting the scoop about what was going on inside the Gold Rush. Overcoming the best efforts of Tony and his security company, agents were able to bug the store and tap its telephones.

Suspicions of problems within the police department were quickly confirmed when the voices of Blasko and Leone were heard informing the bad guys of the law's plans, including surveillance by both the feds and the locals. Blasko's voice in particular was recorded on a regular basis communicating with the Spilotro brothers and Herb Blitzstein. The FBI heard the detective providing the identities of undercover operatives and informants, descriptions of vehicles used by surveillance personnel, and background information on loanshark custom-ers. Stationed outside the Gold Rush in his police car, Blasko telephoned in such messages as, "It's clear," or "They've been tailing him," as the police dispatcher talked in the background. He also made progress reports on his efforts to fix traffic tickets and get charges dropped. These revelations placed a serious strain on the working relationship between the federal and the local cops.

In addition to Blasko and Leone, agents were picking up other useful and interesting information. Tony Spilotro himself was taped coaching grand-jury witnesses before their appearances and taking calls from organized-crime figures from across the country. He also had contact with celebrities, including actor Robert Conrad and singer Barbara McNair. No evidence was produced of any wrongdoing on their part.

Interestingly, in 1972, McNair had married a guy named Rick Manzie. Manzie was described by the Chicago press as a "two-bit minor league toady" of the Chicago Outfit. Mobster-turned-informant Jimmy "the Weasel" Fratiano claimed that Tony had "bought a piece of Barbara," giving him a vested interest in her success. But McNair's new husband was a heroin addict and the newlyweds were both arrested for possession of drugs later that year. The busts made headlines and the negative publicity posed a threat to the singer's future. In the years following, Manzie's addiction continued and he ran up gambling debts at some of the Outfit-controlled casinos. In December 1976, Manzie was found murdered in his Las Vegas home, shot in the head at close range by a small-caliber handgun. His killing was never solved.

By the middle of June, after 79 days of wiretaps, 8,000 conversations had been recorded on 298 tapes. The FBI had amassed enough evidence to obtain search warrants for 83 locations. On June 19, the warrants were executed simultaneously, one of them at the Gold Rush. As agents converged on his store, Tony Spilotro bolted out the door and headed for his home a short distance away. Arriving at the house a few steps ahead of the G-men, he said he wouldn't admit them until his lawyer arrived. The standoff lasted long enough for Tony to contact his attorney, Oscar Goodman, and to make sure certain incriminating items disappeared. In his biography *Of Rats and Men*, Goodman is quoted as saying of his client's actions that day, "He ran into his house ... and there was plenty in the home the FBI would have been interested in ... but Tony held them at bay. He held sixteen FBI agents at bay all by himself while things were happening in the house to make sure that they came up with zip, which was exactly what they came up with."

According to the *Los Angeles Times*, though, the searches, including the one of Tony's house, were productive. Agents described the Gold Rush as "a veritable warehouse of stolen property" and said that a large percentage of its inventory came from a nationwide burglary and fencing ring. Some 4,000 pieces of jewelry were seized from the store, of which 1,400 were later identified as being stolen.

From Tony's house, the police removed communications equipment, a handgun, handcuffs, stock certificates, confidential police intelligence reports, $6,000 in cash, even a private investigator's report on Lefty Rosenthal's activities.

The raid on John Spilotro's house produced $196,045 in paper money, as well as financial records. Safety-deposit boxes belonging to the Spilotro brothers, Herb Blitzstein, and the Gold Rush contained rare coins in mint condition, $20 gold pieces, jewelry, bonds, and $40,000 in cash.

The feds had collected a lot of stuff, items that might have led to convictions and prison time for Tony and his boys. That was not to be, though. A U.S. magistrate later ruled that the raiding agents had gone far beyond the scope authorized in the search warrants and that nearly all the evidence gathered was inadmissible. Chalk up another victory for the Ant. But a downside arrived later in the year: In October, Tony's name was added to Nevada's Black Book, barring him from all casinos.

As for the two rogue cops, after the raids Blasko was fired and overtly went to work for Spilotro. Leone retired for health reasons and moved back to New Jersey. Both men were later indicted for their actions, but neither stood trial. Charges against Leone were dropped due to his deteriorating health. Blasko's case was dismissed due to evidentiary problems.

The impact of the resulting scandal, however, was far-reaching within the law-enforcement community. Other agencies treated the Vegas police like lepers, refusing to interact with them. National organizations declined to grant the locals membership because of their apparent inability to protect sensitive intelligence information. But the cops weren't the only ones with image problems. The FBI's Las Vegas office had also come under fire for alleged inappropriate conduct.

Compromising Comps

Starting in the late 1960s, the word within federal law-enforcement circles was that agents working out of the FBI's Las Vegas office were "freeloading" all over town. They were reportedly receiving free meals and drinks from the very individuals and casinos they were supposed to be investigating or keeping an eye on.

Richard Crane, head of the federal organized-crime strike force in Southern California and Nevada from 1970 to 1975, knew that this conduct, if true, had to be confronted and rectified. Crane complained to Justice Department officials in Washington and an inspection team was sent to Las Vegas to find out what was going on. After a couple of weeks the inspectors left, having supposedly chastised the offending agents. Crane was satisfied—until he began receiving word that the inspection team itself had taken advantage of the available comps! He heard reports that the investigators had enjoyed their stay and left without accomplishing anything; meanwhile, the agents assigned locally were continuing to take advantage of casino largesse. An Internal Revenue Service agent Crane trusted confirmed the allegations. Crane again complained to Washington, but when he left government service in 1975, the problems in Las Vegas continued unchecked.

Jack Keith, agent in charge of the Vegas office from 1974 until 1977, discussed the situation with a *Los Angeles Times* reporter after his retirement. "The precedent was set by one of the first agents in charge in Las Vegas. When he ate at a casino, he never even signed the check. He just got up and left."

Keith offered an explanation of why things got out of hand. "The town was a cesspool. The atmosphere permeated everything. The old-timers were part of it and didn't even know it. No man should have been allowed to stay in that town for more than three years. Some of the agents had been there for ten or fifteen years. I told them there was no such thing as a free lunch and that some day they'd have to pay for it."

But allegations of taking a few meals or seeing some free shows weren't the end of it. Things got worse. When the Dunes and later the Aladdin were wiretapped, the men being taped were content to discuss golf, the weather, and women.

Some of the agents working the taps believed that the lack of productivity was due to leaks originating from other agents. Similar to the situation the police found themselves in, other FBI field offices became reluctant to share information with their Vegas colleagues.

Another complaint to Washington resulted in yet another inspection team being sent to Sin City, in June 1977. This time the investigators weren't compromised. Within a few months, a dozen local agents were censured or reassigned, or opted for early retirement. This housecleaning set the stage for the success of the battles yet to be waged.

Working for "The Man"

What was it like to work for Allen Glick's Argent Corporation when it controlled the Stardust and other casinos? One woman who was in a unique position to know shared her experiences in a 2004 interview. To help protect her privacy, I refer to her as "Connie."

Connie arrived in Las Vegas in August 1969. Within a couple of weeks, the 23-year-old had gotten her first casino job in the payroll department of the Thunderbird Hotel & Casino. She was later transferred to the accounting department, where she made the arrangements for guests who were visiting the hotel on room, food, and beverage comps and handled casino credit for all the junkets. This gave her an opportunity to learn how casinos operated from marketing and customer-service standpoints and to work with some of the best professionals in the field. In 1972, Connie went to work for Circus Circus, adding to her knowledge of the casino business and customer service. In 1976, she accepted a position in the accounting department of Argent's corporate office, located in the Stardust. This turned out to be a turning point in her casino career.

"In those days Las Vegas was a warm friendly escape for fun and relaxation, a place that catered to your every whim.

Customer service was the buzz phrase then. The casinos didn't care about the bottom line in the areas of food, beverage, or rooms. It was the numbers from the gaming operations that counted," Connie recalled.

"It was truly the best time to live in the city of gambling, entertainment, and twenty-four-hour fun. There was an ambience then that has since been lost, an atmosphere that set Vegas apart as the entertainment capital of the world."

Connie's talents were soon noticed by her immediate boss, Frank Mooney. "One morning, Mr. Mooney called me into his office. He said that I was one of his most valued and talented employees and my abilities had come to the attention of others. Frank Rosenthal had contacted him and asked that I be transferred to the marketing department, to work for Martin Black, Argent's Vice President of Marketing. Mr. Mooney said he hated to lose me, but my outgoing personality made me a natural for the new position and it would be an exceptional opportunity for me."

Connie accepted the transfer and soon realized that she'd found her niche. "It was an interesting office, to say the least. A girlfriend of one of the well-known wiseguys worked there. Well ... she didn't really work. She spent most of her time filing her nails, but she collected a nice paycheck.

"After about six months, Martin Black left the company and I took over his position. In those days, there were no female casino executives in Las Vegas. It was a man's world and a good-old-boy town. Women had their place in accounting, secretarial, or food and beverage service, but *never* in a decision-making position in the casino industry. I was the first."

Initially, Connie heard comments from her peers that she had bed-hopped her way up the career ladder. When the more curious ones asked how she'd attained her promotion, she answered, "My brains aren't in my ass; they're in my head." Those kinds of questions quickly faded as Connie proved to be extremely competent in her new position.

Connie worked closely with Lefty Rosenthal and was put in charge of his weekly television show. "It was a delightful challenge and a very exciting experience. I handled all aspects of the show," she recalled.

"My father was my first mentor and Mr. Rosenthal became my second. He gave me opportunities that no one else would have ever given me. He was a perfectionist in every sense of the word, but a very fair person. He was soft-spoken and always treated me with the utmost respect. I met his wife frequently. She was a beautiful woman and was always a lady when I was around her. I will always hold Mr. Rosenthal in the highest esteem."

On paper, Allen Glick was the boss of Argent. But one particular incident proved to Connie who the *real* boss was and how protective Rosenthal could be of those he liked.

"One day I was asked to fly to San Diego to do some editing on our first television show. Upon returning the next day, I was called into Mr. Glick's office. He wanted to know where I had been and who gave me permission to go. I told him. He was anything but nice as he gave me the choice of never again doing what Mr. Rosenthal asked me to do or being fired. I'm sure my loyalty to Mr. Rosenthal was evident to Mr. Glick. But as a young single mother with two children to support, his words scared me and my mind went into freeze mode. I didn't know what to do and stewed over it the rest of the day.

"That evening as I was leaving the casino, I passed Mr. Rosenthal and several of his associates, who were on their way to the Moby Dick restaurant, their favorite place to meet in the Stardust. Mr. Rosenthal said hello to me and I replied back, but without my usual enthusiasm or smile.

"After taking a few more steps, I heard my name called. I turned around and Mr. Rosenthal motioned me over to him; he wanted to know if everything was okay. I told him no, it wasn't. I explained about my session with Mr. Glick. Mr. Rosenthal then asked me to come with him to the Moby Dick.

"Inside the restaurant he had the maitre d' bring a phone to our table. He called Mr. Glick, who had already returned to his home in La Jolla, California. The conversation from Mr. Rosenthal's end went like this: 'Good evening, Allen. I hear that you had Connie come to your office today on a matter that doesn't really concern you. We need to get something straight, Allen. I run things around here; Connie works for me, not you. And if you ever approach her or threaten to fire her again, I'll break both of your legs. Do you understand? That's good. Good evening, Allen.' He hung up the phone and told me I didn't have to worry about anything like that happening again. From that point on, Mr. Glick never bothered me again. In fact, he didn't even speak to me."

For Connie, what had been her dream job ended when Argent was dismantled as a result of the casino skimming investigations. She was a target of the Gaming Control Board for a period of time and was called to testify. She was eventually dropped from the investigation and wasn't charged with any wrongdoing.

After Argent, Connie opened up the Sundance Hotel & Casino in July 1980 for Moe Dalitz, who owned the Sundance. Connie found him to be a kind man, one with wealth and power, but you'd never know it.

To Connie, her days of working for the "family" were the best of her life. "I have fond memories of those days. It was an exciting fairy-tale experience for me. Unlike the megaresorts of today, customer service was a priority. And that's the way it should be."

Lefty's Licensing Woes

While Tony Spilotro approached his goal of ruling organized crime in Las Vegas, successfully navigating through mine fields along the way, Lefty Rosenthal's climb to the top of the casino industry proved more difficult. A few years after his move to the Stardust, his current and past association with the criminal element came back to haunt him.

The trouble began in 1974, when Rosenthal applied for a gaming work card. Unfortunately for him, applicants deemed to be key employees of a casino were subjected to rigorous background investigations, with their friends and associates receiving special scrutiny. Lefty's relationship to Tony Spilotro and the Chicago Outfit sealed his fate. His application was initially denied, but an appeal of the decision was decided in Lefty's favor. Then the Nevada Supreme Court upheld a lower court's ruling that the denial of Rosenthal's application had been hasty and that he'd been deprived of his ability to hold a key casino position without prior notice or the opportunity to be heard. But the reprieve was only temporary.

The Nevada Legislature quickly passed legislation mandating that anyone found to be unqualified for a gaming license couldn't be employed by, or have any contact with, a casino licensee except as an entertainer. In an attempt to sidestep the whole licensing issue, Lefty gave himself the non-gaming title of Food & Beverage Director. When that description didn't fly, he became Entertainment Director.

To partially justify the latter title, Lefty taped a weekly variety show at the Stardust that was broadcast by a local TV station on Saturday evenings. "The Frank Rosenthal Show" was described by some as surreal and by others as horrible, but it drew an audience. Guests included such celebrities of the day as Frank Sinatra, O.J. Simpson, and Frankie Valli, along with a bookmaker or two. Lefty offered comments about his ongoing fight with, and his less than flattering opinion of, the Gaming Control Board. Although some viewers found Lefty's antics humorous, others weren't amused. The Outfit, craving anonymity for their Las Vegas operations, now had *two* apparently loose cannons making lots of news: Tony and Lefty. On top of that, Nick Civella, head of the Kansas City Mob, which was receiving money from the casino skim, felt that Rosenthal was getting too chummy with the FBI and might "flip" if the going got tough.

Gaming regulators and law enforcement didn't believe for a minute that Rosenthal's activities at the Stardust were confined to the entertainment department. They were sure he was the Outfit's inside man and that Allen Glick was the front man. The legal and public-relations clashes between the two sides continued. In June 1978, Gaming Control again told Lefty that his duties required him to obtain a gaming license. The hearings over Lefty's status and eligibility to be licensed turned increasingly heated as Rosenthal, in frequent outbursts, attacked the Gaming Commission and its chairman, Harry Reid, now a United States Senator, in the most colorful terms. Career-wise, the whole episode turned out to be a disaster for Lefty—he was not only refused a license, but his name also joined Tony Spilotro's in the infamous Black Book. He was out of the casino business and, thanks to being "booked," couldn't even set foot inside a gaming establishment. Subsequent appeals of the Commission's actions failed. But for the Outfit, it wasn't all that bad. Although they lost their inside man, they still had Allen Glick. And Lefty could be replaced.

As bad as this turn of events was for Lefty professionally, it paled in comparison to what was going on in his personal life.

The Rift

Lefty couldn't have been particularly happy when Tony Spilotro showed up in Las Vegas, knowing the potential impact of their relationship on his future licensing possibilities. Those concerns proved to be well-founded. But for the up-and-coming gaming tycoon, they weren't the worst of it.

The first four years of marriage had been fruitful for the Rosenthals. They had two children, first Stephen and then Stephanie. Lefty's position at the Stardust came with a hefty contract. Geri lived the good life and money was no object. On the surface, their lives seemed nearly ideal. But behind the façade, Geri Rosenthal was an unhappy woman. She entered into matrimony somewhat reluctantly and as time passed, she seemed to regret that decision.

When Lefty's professional life became difficult as he fought the gaming regulators, his children provided an escape from the stress. Both youngsters were natural swimmers. Geri and Lefty spent a lot of time working with them in the family swimming pool on hot desert afternoons. The kids eventually became members of the Las Vegas Sandpipers swim team. The proud parents attended all of their tournaments and the doting father served as the official announcer at the meets, except for the races in which his children participated. When Rosenthal was ousted from the casino business in 1978, he remained upbeat, calling the decision a "blessing in disguise," as it allowed him to devote more time to Stephen and Stephanie.

While the children provided solace for Lefty, the same couldn't be said of Geri. She'd become increasingly disgruntled with her situation, drinking to excess, taking drugs, and frequently staying out all night. Lefty was concerned about her behavior for more than one reason. In addition to the strain her conduct was placing on their marriage, on a professional level he had to worry about whom she was spending her time with and what she was saying to them. Lefty, after all, held a powerful position in the gaming industry, operating in the shadowy world of organized crime. His enemies or rivals could use his wife to obtain information to blackmail him. And the law … always lurking in the background … had an army of undercover operatives and informants with their noses to the ground in pursuit of usable intelligence. To help him keep track of Geri, Lefty demanded that she carry a mobile phone with her at all times. For Geri, the situation was becoming intolerable.

As if the Gaming Control Board, the law, and his wife

weren't causing the oddsmaker enough grief, his old buddy Tony Spilotro was now running amok. Lefty encouraged Tony to keep a low profile, but the Ant seemed intent not only on expanding his criminal empire, but actually hogging the law-enforcement and media spotlight. In fact, Tony wanted Lefty's full support in his efforts. When Rosenthal refused, the relationship between the two men grew tense at best.

And then it happened. In July 1978, right on the heels of his gaming license being denied, Geri admitted to her husband that she was having an affair. That news was bad enough. Worse yet, her lover was none other than Tony Spilotro himself. Lefty must have been angry and hurt, but he was also scared. He made Geri promise not to tell Spilotro that she had confessed. There was no telling what the bosses in Chicago would do if they discovered their Las Vegas enforcer had become involved with their embattled inside-man's wife.

Tony would certainly know that and with the relationship between him and Lefty already deteriorating, he'd fear that the aggrieved husband might make a complaint to Chicago. Lefty knew that people who posed a threat to Tony tended to have a brief life expectancy. He told Geri that if the volatile Spilotro learned Lefty knew the truth, he'd probably kill them both. They had no choice but to continue on as though nothing were wrong. It would be difficult, but their lives probably depended on it.

So, while Lefty struggled under his many burdens, Tony Spilotro cruised along, seemingly immune from being taken to task for any of his alleged wrongdoings. In fact, the Ant was simultaneously extending his influence and laying the groundwork for future expansion—westward.

The California Connection

Although Tony Spilotro was based in Las Vegas, his mob-related duties weren't limited to Sin City or Nevada.

He was also active in neighboring California, specifically Los Angeles, where he carried out the instructions he received from Chicago. Los Angeles did have its own crime family, but the Chicago Outfit held it in low esteem. For years, the City of Angels gangsters, referred to as the "Mickey Mouse Mafia," had been tolerated by the Chicago bosses, who did pretty much what they wanted to in Los Angeles, but hadn't actually taken total control of organized crime there. Tony wasn't the first mobster to do Chicago's bidding in the Southwest, though. Another man had been there before him.

The underworld relationship between Chicago and Los Angeles went back to the Capone days, when Scarface Al had sent a hood named Johnny Roselli out west to look after Chicago's interests. Other Capone men had preceded Roselli and had already infiltrated the Alliance of Theatrical Stage Employees, the union backbone of the movie business. Johnny settled in Beverly Hills, married actress June Lang, and became friends with many of the film industry's most influential people. One of his pals was Harry Cohn, president of Columbia Pictures. Cohn later testified that his relationship with Roselli kept Columbia virtually free from labor problems.

Other studios decided not to cozy up to the Chicagoans, however, and they experienced a tougher time keeping their facilities up and running. Roselli and company offered to help bring labor peace to these uncooperative companies for a price. The amount was reportedly $1 million. But the intended victims didn't just roll over and pay the money; they reported the attempted shakedown to the law.

Johnny and an associate named Willie Bioff were convicted in 1944 and sentenced to 10 years in prison. Paroled in three years, Roselli returned to Hollywood and took positions as an associate producer and consultant to several studios. It was almost as though the conviction never happened.

With legalized gambling then beginning to take off in Las Vegas, Roselli extended his influence out to the desert. Within a few years he was able to have waitresses and dealers hired or fired with a phone call and arrange for casino executives to be canned for failing to show him proper respect. He also became the man to contact if you needed a comped room or the best seats for shows at Strip properties, such as the Dunes or the Flamingo.

Roselli was a slender man, with snow-white hair and a penchant for wearing dark glasses. After divorcing June Lang, he developed a reputation as a ladies' man. His female companions included such starlets and other notables as Judith Exner, who later wrote a book claiming affairs with President John Kennedy and Roselli's Chicago boss, Sam Giancana. His power was such that the CIA recruited both him and Giancana in 1960 to participate in a plot to assassinate Fidel Castro. In the 1960s, Johnny Roselli was indeed a man to be reckoned with.

The beginning of the end of Roselli's reign as Chicago's top man in Los Angeles and Las Vegas—and the opening for Tony Spilotro—started in 1969. He and three others were convicted in connection with a major card-cheating scam at the Friars Club in Beverly Hills. Victims of the scheme included millionaire industrialists such as Theodore Briskin, celebrity comedians Zeppo Marx and Phil Silvers, and singer Tony Martin. That conviction earned Roselli a five-year prison sentence. Around the same time he was called before a federal grand jury investigating allegations of organized-crime influence in several Las Vegas casinos. In spite of being granted immunity for his testimony, Roselli claimed he told the grand jury nothing. Roselli's denial may or may not have been truthful, but the subsequent jailing of three Mafia figures led Chicago to doubt his sincerity. Over the years, many gangsters have learned that even being suspected of having loose lips can eventually prove fatal.

Roselli was released from prison in 1973. Seeking to reestablish himself, he sought the help of the Los Angeles gangsters he'd been friendly with. Unfortunately for the ex-con, the L.A. family was down to about a dozen members, compared to the 200 or 300 in families located in cities of comparable size. The Mickey Mouse Mafia wasn't in a position to help Roselli, or anyone else. To add to his problem, he was also aware that while he was incarcerated, a new tough guy named Tony Spilotro had moved into Las Vegas.

In desperation, Roselli turned to an old friend, Aladena "Jimmy the Weasel" Fratiano. Although he lived in the San Francisco area and not Los Angeles, the Weasel was a former West Coast enforcer for the mob who reputedly had 12 notches on his gun. But Roselli was out of luck again; Fratiano was also on the outs with the mob. In his book *The Last Mafioso*, Fratiano recalls a conversation during a dinner meeting with Roselli at a Tony Roma's restaurant in Los Angeles in 1974.

Fratiano: "Spilotro's got your old job in Vegas. You know, arbitrating beefs like you did in the old days. He's doing things you never did. He's shylocking, has a crew of burglars working ..."

Roselli, cutting in: "Spilotro's a watchdog for Joe Aiuppa. But this guy's an animal, a punk with no class, no finesse. He's just a soldier. He's Aiuppa's messenger boy, a tool, but I hear he's acting tough. You can't play tough in that town and last."

Fratiano: "But he's also a worker. This guy's clipped [murdered] some people."

Roselli: "Sure. If Aiuppa wants any work done in this end of the country, he gets Tony and tells him to go ahead and take care of it."

In two years Johnny Roselli's number was up. The gangster left his sister's home in Florida on July 28, 1976. Ten days later his remains were found in a 55-gallon drum floating in Miami's Biscayne Bay. Apparently, Roselli's lanky body had been a tough fit; his legs had been chopped off and stuffed into the barrel alongside his head and torso. Like many gangland killings, Roselli's murder was never solved. Regardless of who was responsible for it, Roselli's death clearly benefited Tony Spilotro. No one was left in Southern California to undermine his authority.

Fratiano himself went on to become an annoyance to the Outfit. He turned into a swaggering loudmouth, bragging that he was the toughest mobster in California. He attempted to muscle a Beverly Hills lawyer with mob ties, allegedly putting a dead fish in the attorney's mailbox to intimidate him.

Fratiano was summoned to Chicago for a face-to-face with Doves Aiuppa. Warned to clean up his act, he was allowed to return to California. Rather than follow those orders, however, Fratiano instead boasted that he planned to hustle money from some rich Las Vegas gamblers who were old friends of the Chicago bosses. That proved to be an unwise move. As far as Chicago was concerned, enough was enough. The Weasel had to go.

By 1977, Fratiano was sure he was a marked man. He was also convinced that Johnny Roselli's replacement, Tony Spilotro, had the contract on him. Criminal associates tried to lure the Weasel back to Chicago, but he didn't go. Another "friend" called and told him he needed to get to a phone booth right away for a confidential call. It was a ruse Fratiano had used himself to get his victim out in the open. He refused to budge. The FBI had Fratiano under surveillance at the time and knew his days were numbered. The feds contacted him and made him an offer he couldn't refuse: Testify against his organized-crime colleagues and enjoy the relative safety of the Witness Protection Program, or await a visit from Spilotro or one of his men. Omerta, the vow of silence, fell by the wayside and Fratiano became a government witness.

According to FBI documents, Fratiano told FBI agents during an April 1978 interview that Tony Spilotro had contacted him and offered $10,000 if he refused to provide prosecutors with information against any of the gangsters the government was pursuing. More money would be forthcoming if he continued to keep silent. Fratiano asked that the $10,000 be paid to his attorney, but the cash was never received. He also confirmed that he believed it was Spilotro's intent to kill him.

Through Fratiano and other informants, the feds opened a second front in their war against Tony.

Teflon Tony

John Gotti, the infamous former head of New York City's Gambino crime family, was dubbed the Teflon Don for his ability to gain acquittals whenever the law took him to court. In fact, from the time he ascended to the throne in 1985 until his conviction in 1992 for violations of the Racketeer Influenced and Corrupt Organizations Act (RICO), Gotti and his lawyers had made a habit out of beating up on prosecutors. But Gotti was finally convicted and served time while he was making his way up the career ladder. And the sentence for his only conviction while he was the boss was a beauty: life without the possibility of parole.

Although Tony Spilotro never officially attained "Don" status, the attention he received from the law was nearly the same as that bestowed on higher-ranking mobsters. In spite of being almost continuously under investigation and a suspect in some 25 murders and countless other felonies, Tony conducted his affairs for more than a decade without being convicted of even a minor offense. Part of the reason for that impressive run could be his skills as a criminal; another likely factor was that his reputation and willingness to use violence made witnesses against him scarce. A third and equally important aspect was his lawyer, Oscar Goodman.

Goodman was born in Philadelphia and graduated from the University of Pennsylvania Law School. After moving to Las Vegas in 1964, he opened his own law practice. It wasn't long before he became one of the city's premier criminal defense attorneys, representing many high-profile clients. Among them were Harry Claiborne, a federal judge who was convicted of tax evasion in 1983 and impeached by the United States Senate, Allen Glick and his Argent Corporation, Lefty Rosenthal, and Tony Spilotro.

Goodman was a fiery advocate for his clients and he wasn't shy about attacking his law-enforcement foes, both in and out of court. In *Of Rats and Men*, author John L. Smith chronicles the life and career of Oscar Goodman. At the beginning of that book are quotes from several people, including two from Goodman that may illustrate his attitude toward his opponents and the existence of organized crime. "I'd rather have my daughter date Tony Spilotro than an FBI agent," and "There is no mob."

Whether these words accurately reflected Mr. Goodman's feelings or were only issued for public consumption, one can imagine that Tony, Allen, and Lefty appreciated hearing their legal representative say such things. But Goodman wasn't merely rhetoric; he produced for those who placed their trust in him.

Together, Tony and Oscar, each using his own unique talents, made a team that prosecutors seemed unable to beat.

On The Home Front

As busy as he was, Tony wasn't on the job 24/7. As a former Las Vegas TV reporter told me, "Tony didn't spend all his time whacking and hacking." He did have a wife and son. In an effort to find out if there was another side to the Ant, I spoke with Nancy and Vincent Spilotro. Per agreement, Tony's business activities were not discussed.

According to Nancy Spilotro, her husband was a regular guy. He liked home cooking and they seldom ate out. Tony's own culinary skills were limited to fixing their son breakfast, usually consisting of pancakes. As a couple, they seldom visited the Strip unless there was a special show they wanted to see or if they were acting as tour guides for out-of-town company. The family visited Disneyland from time to time, where Tony's favorite ride was "It's A Small World." *The Sound of Music*, with Julie Andrews, was his favorite movie. He was no "Mr. Fix It" and wasn't particularly handy around the house. The Spilotros lived comfortably, but not flamboyantly.

Prior to speaking with Vincent, I reviewed an article called "Growing Up Spilotro," that appeared in the November 2003 issue of *Las Vegas Life*. During our several telephone conversations in the first few months of 2004, we discussed the content of that piece. "He was the most loving man I ever knew," Vincent Spilotro told me, repeating a quote from the magazine.

Vincent remembers life as being good as he grew up in Las Vegas. He recalls his father taking him on Colorado River trips, sometimes in the company of casino owners. Other times the two of them just went cruising around town. In his son's eyes, the alleged mob enforcer was honest and generous, willing to give advice to neighborhood kids. There were also the times his father couldn't get to sleep unless Vincent put his arm around him. "He only slept a couple of hours a night. Having my arm around him helped."

But he also has memories of raids by federal agents and a shooting incident at his house when he was 14. On that occasion, someone attacked his home, and his uncle John's house, which was located just down the street, with shotguns. Although some shotgun pellets came uncomfortably close to the teenager's head, no one was injured during the assault. The building and his mother's car were damaged, however. No one was ever charged in the incident, but both Vincent and his mother believe the police were the culprits.

His father's reputation gave a unique character to his experiences in school. The other kids knew about Tony and gave Vincent appropriate respect. "I couldn't get in a fight if I tried," he says. And his girlfriends didn't dare cheat on him. Sometimes Tony brought celebrities, such as actor Robert Conrad, to his son's baseball games, making the boy a celebrity in his own right. A few teachers even asked Vincent if he would get Tony's autograph for them.

According to Sister Lorraine Forster, who knew Vincent as a student at Bishop Gorman High School, the boy was no problem. "He was a handsome young man," the retired nun remembers. "He didn't cause any trouble, didn't bring any attention to himself. If anything, I'd say he was quiet, maybe a little shy. He was a nice kid."

But young Vincent also lived by a code of silence. "If I knew someone had done something wrong, I couldn't tell on them. That's the way it was." And sometimes Tony would advise him that the father of one of his classmates was an informant and to be careful. It was not the life of a typical student, to be sure.

Vincent doesn't try to portray his father as a saint, but neither does he believe the way Tony is portrayed in books and movies is accurate. He doesn't think his father was capable of that kind of violence, or that he ever killed anybody. "I just can't see it," he said.

Was Tony Spilotro a vicious mobster or a loving husband and doting father? Depending on one's perspective, he might have been both.

The Tide Turns

Tony's first seven years in Las Vegas were eventful, to say the least. He was firmly entrenched as the King of the Strip and his tentacles reached into California. Money was coming in from a variety of illegal sources. Allegations of criminal acts rolled off him like water off a duck's back. The federal and local agencies investigating him each had image problems and didn't necessarily trust each other on the organizational level. The law seemingly was unable to lay a glove on him. It was true that his relationship with Lefty Rosenthal had gone sour, but the one with his former friend's wife was perking along and, to his knowledge, wasn't known to the oddsmaker. All seemed to be good in the Ant's realm.

But his victories over the law were only the initial skirmishes. The battle was far from over; in fact, it was only beginning. Things were happening in the law-enforcement arena that soon began to turn the tide. The FBI was making personnel moves and preparing to launch a full-court press to take Tony down. And in November 1978, Clark County voters made a change at the top of their police department, electing a reform candidate who had vowed to put Tony and his gang in jail or run them out of town.

It was time for round two.

6

The Law

By 1978, the population of the Las Vegas Valley had increased to more than 400,000. The tourist numbers were also up dramatically from 1970, nearly doubling to 11 million. Construction of new housing and commercial buildings flourished. With all the long- and short-term arrivals, small-town Las Vegas was gradually but steadily disappearing. And along with the people came their money, improving the economy for the honest and dishonest alike.

The structure of local law enforcement had also undergone a major makeover since Tony Spilotro's arrival in Las Vegas. On July 1, 1973, the Las Vegas Police Department and the Clark County Sheriff's Department merged to form the Las Vegas Metropolitan Police Department. Metro, as it became known, was the largest police agency in Nevada. Its jurisdiction covered 8,000 square miles and included the city of Las Vegas and the rest of sprawling unincorporated Clark County. As a part of the initial organizational setup, Clark County Sheriff Ralph Lamb headed the new department. The Lamb family was a powerful political force in the state, and Ralph Lamb, known as "Mr. Metro," had been the top lawman in Clark

County since 1961. His second in command was Undersheriff John Moran, former Las Vegas Chief of Police.

The consolidation itself had been difficult to implement and was unpopular with many police officers, deputies, and politicians. Institutional and personal rivalries festered for the first several months after the merger. In addition to those problems, Metro was initially plagued by budget woes and a lack of equipment, resulting in officers wearing the uniforms and sidearms of their former departments and driving the old vehicles. These ingredients were contrary to a unified police agency.

Metro survived that rocky start and eventually obtained the financing and equipment it needed. In a short time morale began to improve and the animosities of the past were left behind, at least as far as the officers were concerned. Some politicians didn't forget so quickly, however. Attempts to deconsolidate Metro continued from time to time for years to come.

The fledgling agency had other difficulties, too. Rumors circulated of corruption within the department, and that Sheriff Lamb himself was less than honest. In 1977, Lamb was indicted on charges of income-tax evasion. The IRS alleged that Lamb spent more money than he earned and had accepted "loans" from casino owner Benny Binion—loans that were never intended to be repaid.

The tarnished image of the department didn't sit well with some, including Commander John McCarthy, head of the Vice, Narcotics and Juvenile Bureau. The New Jersey native and former Las Vegas Police Department cop decided to do something about it: challenge his boss—the nearly legendary Ralph Lamb—in the 1978 election. It was a bold decision, to say the least. Had Lefty Rosenthal handicapped McCarthy's chances of beating Lamb at that early point, he would likely have made him a substantial underdog. But, odds aside, McCarthy had made up his mind.

John McCarthy

John D. McCarthy was born in Weehawken, New Jersey, on March 4, 1934. His father died when he was seven and times were tough financially. The young McCarthy earned spending money selling newspapers on the street and shining shoes in the local bars. As a teen he got a job at the Gibraltar Paper Box Company, going to high school during the day and working the afternoon shift at the plant. After paying his mother $15 per week for room and board, he was able to save enough money to buy a car.

Upon completing high school in 1952, McCarthy took a better paying job at the General Motors Assembly Plant in Linden, New Jersey, about 20 miles from his home. But the Korean War was still raging, and knowing he was likely to be drafted at any time, he elected to enlist in the Marine Corps in 1953. Hostilities in Korea ended while McCarthy was still undergoing infantry training at Camp Pendleton, California. He was subsequently assigned to the Marine base at Lake Mead, Nevada, and spent the next 18 months guarding some of America's deadliest weapons.

During his tour in Nevada, he met a girl and fell in love. When he was discharged in February 1956, he headed back to New Jersey, but vowed to return as soon as he saved some money. True to his word, McCarthy was back five months later.

The ex-Marine took a job as a mechanic for the Las Vegas, Tonopah & Reno Bus Line. One day while he was servicing a bus, a Las Vegas police car pulled up. The officer behind the wheel was one of his former Marine Corps buddies; he asked McCarthy if he'd ever considered getting into police work. Later that same day the cop returned with an application for his friend to fill out. Within a few weeks McCarthy had taken and passed a civil service test and a physical exam. He was hired as a police officer on September 13, 1956.

The new cop was issued a couple of used uniforms and was loaned a .38 revolver, handcuffs, and leather gear. His pay was $360 per month, which figured out to $2.25 an hour. There was no provision for overtime pay at that time.

McCarthy had gained a new job, but shortly after being hired he and his girlfriend split up. He wasn't unattached for long, though. While on patrol one night, he handled a call that led to a stop at Memorial, the town's only hospital in those days. While there he met a nurse, Marjorie McHale, and began dating her almost immediately. They were married in January 1958. Their first son, Michael, was born on July 3, 1959. A second son, Brian, was born on June 2, 1962.

On the job, McCarthy moved from patrol duty to the Detective Bureau in 1961. He worked the burglary and robbery details. At that time his shift supervisor was also the chief homicide investigator. As a result, McCarthy assisted in the investigation of 24 homicides that year.

In 1963, McCarthy's mother passed away. While he was back in New Jersey for her funeral, he met a childhood friend who was then a lieutenant with the Union City Police Department. They'd each been with their respective agencies for about the same amount of time, yet his friend had already been promoted twice. When he asked his pal how he had attained rank in such a relatively short time, he got this answer: His buddy had purchased source books for the formulation of questions for police promotional exams and made up questions and answers that he wrote on 3x5 cards. He carried the cards with him while on patrol and studied them religiously when he wasn't on a call. He became a well-prepared test taker and his efforts had paid off.

Although he'd never been an enthusiastic student, McCarthy decided that when he returned to Las Vegas, he'd do the same thing his friend had done. He kept the promise he'd made to himself and was promoted to sergeant later that year. In 1964, he was named to head the department's vice and narcotics detail. A promotion to lieutenant followed in 1968. In 1974, now with Metro, he attained the rank of captain. The following year marked another advancement when he was appointed Commander of the Vice, Narcotics and Juvenile Bureau.

By 1977, Commander McCarthy was disillusioned with the leadership of his boss, Ralph Lamb. Sheriff Lamb was under investigation by the IRS. One of Lamb's brothers was a partner in a bar supply business that had won a contract with almost every resort hotel in the Valley. Lamb himself sat on the Clark County Liquor & Gaming Board and cast votes on the suitability of applicants on whom his own officers conducted background investigations. On top of that, there were rumors that some cops in the Intelligence Bureau were on the mob's payroll. To McCarthy, these situations represented conflicts of interest at the least and possible criminal activity at the worst. Metro's credibility with the valley's citizens and other law-enforcement agencies was in jeopardy. In his mind, the only sure way to reverse the damage to his department's reputation was to make a change at the top. With that motivation, John McCarthy decided to toss his hat into the political ring.

Recruiting Support

Gary Lang was born and raised in Las Vegas. In 1965, while working as a police cadet in the Las Vegas Police Department, he became a friend of John McCarthy. After a stint in the Army, he rejoined the police department for a short time as a civilian Identification Technician before attending college, obtaining a law degree from the University of Utah, and returning to Southern Nevada.

In the 1970s, he was a practicing criminal defense attorney. His duties frequently brought him to the Metro offices in the City Hall complex on Stewart Avenue. On one such visit in 1977, Lang was walking by McCarthy's office when the Vice

& Narcotics chief asked him to step inside and close the door. "I've decided to run against Ralph Lamb in the election next year," the cop announced.

"The first thing I asked him," Lang recalls, "was if there was any way I could talk him out of it. He said there wasn't; his mind was made up. McCarthy said he was looking for an advisor and wanted to know if I'd be interested. I accepted his offer."

In April 1978, McCarthy approached the Clark County Republican Party and won support for his candidacy. He filed the necessary paperwork the following month. He presented himself as a reform candidate, vowing to restore Metro's reputation and prestige. Although Sheriff Lamb was acquitted of the tax charges in federal court, those and other allegations, along with the revelations about Detective Joe Blasko and Sgt. Phil Leone, had taken their toll. John McCarthy defeated "Mr. Metro" at the ballot box that November. The celebration was short-lived, however. Though it was difficult beating Ralph Lamb, the next four years proved to be much more so. The problems began immediately.

Promotions, Resentment, and a Lawsuit

Both supporters and critics knew John McCarthy as a first-class honest cop who wanted to do a good job. His integrity wasn't an issue with those who worked with and for him. Those same people also agree that he was politically naïve and not a proponent of the art of compromise; McCarthy was more the type to make decisions based on what he thought was right, stick to his guns, and let the chips fall where they may. One such decision created a firestorm even before he took office.

In order to implement his campaign promises to reform Metro, McCarthy needed people he could trust in positions of authority within the department. That meant, for example, promoting patrolmen and detectives he felt he could rely on to upper-level management positions over others with more seniority, rank, and experience.

Many of the people who felt they deserved promotions had been Lamb supporters and weren't happy with McCarthy's election to begin with. The news that they were being bypassed in favor of what they thought were McCarthy's cronies went over badly. Their reaction wasn't limited to locker-room grumbling. On December 28, 39 Metro officers filed a class-action lawsuit challenging the legality of McCarthy's appointments.

Gary Lang, who had agreed to hold two positions in the new administration, Legal Advisor to Metro and Counsel to the Sheriff, was aware that emotions were running high even before the lawsuit was initiated. On Thanksgiving Day after the election, he received a bomb threat at his residence and was forced to leave his home for two days; no bomb was found. The lawyer isn't sure members of Metro made the threat, though. He believes that many people in Clark County who had benefited from their relationship with Ralph Lamb over the years were threatened by the election results.

Lang litigated the class-action suit on behalf of Sheriff McCarthy. It was his position that, unpopular or not, McCarthy had no choice but to make the promotions he did. And he was confident the Sheriff had the authority to make them. The court found his argument convincing and ruled in McCarthy's favor in January. The case was over, but resentment lingered.

Intelligence Bureau

One of the people McCarthy tapped for advancement was destined to become a key player in the efforts to restore Metro's damaged image, as well as in the fight against Tony Spilotro. Kent Clifford, a former Las Vegas Police Department vice and narcotics detective, had been working for McCarthy at Metro. Clifford was promoted to Commander and put in charge of the Intelligence Bureau. It was a hot-potato assignment, with pressure to produce results almost immediately. Was the appointee up to the task? John McCarthy certainly thought so.

Kent Clifford was born and raised on a farm in Idaho. Upon graduation from high school in 1963, the 18 year old and a buddy left home to make their fortunes, ending up in Las Vegas. Drafted into the Army in 1965, Clifford attended Officer Candidate School. The new Second Lieutenant then spent a year in Germany, where he was promoted to First Lieutenant. That assignment was followed by a 12-month tour in Vietnam, where he was awarded Silver and Bronze stars for his performance in battle. After being discharged, he returned to Las Vegas and enrolled in the University of Nevada at Las Vegas.

Shortly before graduating in 1972, he was sitting in a political science class when the professor started a discussion about the American flag. According to her, the flag was merely a piece of cloth that could be used as a shirt, tablecloth, or rug; even burning it wasn't a problem. Those comments enraged Clifford, who raised his hand and told the professor, "You shouldn't be telling the kids that kind of garbage." As the combat veteran spoke, several students began clapping. His fans turned out to be cops who were enrolled in the same class. Afterward, they invited him to have lunch with them. During conversation Clifford mentioned that he was looking for a job. His new friends suggested that he apply to the Las Vegas Police Department. He'd never considered doing police work and politely declined. A few weeks later, the same group asked Clifford to attend a meeting they set up with Assistant Chief of Police George Allen. Not wanting to hurt anyone's feelings, he agreed. Clifford walked out of that meeting as a newly hired police officer.

Sheriff McCarthy wasn't the only one to think highly of Kent Clifford. Even a McCarthy critic, one of the 39 officers in the class-action lawsuit, described Clifford this way: "He was one hell of an undercover cop, with guts a mile deep." The detectives who worked for Clifford in the reorganized unit quickly developed similar respect for their boss. He was aggressive, fearless, and loyal to his officers. Over the next four years, he needed each of those qualities, and more.

Commander Clifford wasted no time in getting started, tackling the problems head-on in January 1979. He reorganized the Intelligence Bureau through a series of personnel moves and announced that the Bureau was "clean" to the best of his knowledge. In March, Metro was reinstated into the California Narcotics Intelligence Network, an organization from which it had been suspended due to information leaks regarding the Spilotro investigations. As satisfying as that start may have been, another matter needed to be addressed quickly: Tony Spilotro himself.

Targeting Tony

Although Commander Clifford was newly assigned to confront Spilotro, he was well-aware of the gangster's reputation and presence. Clifford described his adversary this way: "Tony Spilotro was a cold-blooded killer. You could see it when you looked into his eyes. He was capable of being extremely vicious and violent."

The former Intelligence boss disagrees with newspaper accounts that killings involving the use of a .22 were the "signature" of the Spilotro gang. "Tony used a twenty-two, but that particular weapon wasn't unique to him. A lot of hit men used a twenty-two." According to Clifford, Spilotro, or men acting on his orders, also murdered with knives, ice picks, or any other weapon that struck their fancy.

In spite of acknowledging Spilotro as a dangerous killer,

Clifford wasn't particularly impressed with the Ant, believing his status was overblown. "He was just a soldier, a punk. That's all he ever was."

Still, Clifford had to develop a strategy on how to deal with Tony. The feds were hot on the trail of Rosenthal, Glick, and the casino skimming operations, as well as Spilotro, so Metro could focus on Spilotro and his street crimes, which fell directly under its jurisdiction. He decided to attack both overtly and covertly. Five officers were assigned full-time to the Spilotro investigation and could be supplemented by additional personnel as needed. They kept pressure on Tony and his associates by implementing round-the-clock surveillance, often making no effort at concealment. The targets knew they were there, watching their every move, even following them into restaurants and taking seats at adjoining tables.

In addition, the tailing cops were told to aggressively enforce traffic laws. When a subject was pulled over for a motor-vehicle violation, he was arrested and had his car towed. This tactic disrupted their activities, costing them time and money, as well as causing annoyance. It also allowed the cops to get positive identifications on the players and possibly pick up some good information. "Some of those guys weren't real bright. You never knew what they might say when they were in the back seat of your car on the way to jail," Clifford said.

Although this strategy invited allegations of police harassment, Clifford believed it was necessary and appropriate. "We were up against people who weren't required to play by any rules; we were. Everything we did was legal, but sometimes we went right up to the edge. The goal was to put Tony in prison or drive him out of town. Also, there was a possibility that by keeping the media's attention focused on him, along with his own huge ego, his bosses in Chicago might eventually get fed up with him."

An additional matter needed to be taken care of in relation to the war against Tony Spilotro. A bond of trust had to be established between Metro and the FBI. On an organizational level, that would take time, a luxury the cops didn't have. Instead, Clifford and his officers developed relationships with their FBI counterparts on a personal basis, building friendships and confidence in one another's abilities. As these efforts came to fruition, cooperation between the two agencies grew. It marked a new phase in the struggle against organized crime in Las Vegas.

The FBI

Metro wasn't alone in making Tony a priority in the late 1970s. The FBI was also beefing up its forces in Vegas, bringing in additional personnel from other offices. Among the new arrivals were Emmett Michaels, Charlie Parsons, Dennis Arnoldy, Lynn Ferrin, Gary Magnesen, and Joseph Yablonsky. All six played key roles in the eventual downfall of the Spilotro gang in Las Vegas and other mobsters across the country in conjunction with the casino skimming investigations.

Emmett Michaels was assigned to the Las Vegas field office in 1977. He was appointed as supervisor of the Surveillance Squad, a part of the Special Operations Group. He held this position until his retirement in 1985. His unit was responsible for conducting surveillance activities, including the installation and monitoring of authorized wiretaps and electronic eavesdropping equipment.

Charlie Parsons got to Vegas in 1979. He was assigned as supervisor of the Organized Crime Squad, a job he kept until he was transferred to the Los Angeles field office in 1984. He later became the special agent in charge (SAC) of that office and retired from that post in 1996 after a 27-year career.

Dennis Arnoldy was assigned to Las Vegas from Little Rock, Arkansas, in August 1980. Upon his arrival he was made co-case agent with special agent Joe Gersky on the Spilotro investigations. When agent Gersky became a polygraph examiner, Arnoldy became the case agent. As part of his duties, he handled the debriefing and interrogation of a Spilotro lieutenant who turned government witness.

Lynn Ferrin was assigned to Las Vegas in September 1980. He became the case agent for the Strawman and Strawman-Trans Sterling investigations that broke the mob's casino skimming operations. He was transferred to Reno in 1995 and retired in 2001 with nearly 29 years of service.

Joseph Yablonsky was transferred to Las Vegas from Cincinnati in 1980 as the new SAC. He remained the FBI's top man in the Vegas office until his retirement in December 1983, with 32 years of service. Yablonski had a proven track record of developing cases against organized-crime figures and was handpicked for the Sin City assignment by FBI Director William Webster. During his term, Yablonski oversaw an operation consisting of 140 employees, 82 of whom were special agents and five were supervisors, and a $5 million annual budget.

Strike Force

In addition, the Organized Crime Strike Force of the Department of Justice—a program established by Attorney General Robert Kennedy in the early 1960s for the sole purpose of fighting organized crime—provided resident Special Attorneys to coordinate investigative efforts between federal agencies, obtain necessary warrants, evaluate evidence, and prosecute cases in the courts. The unit had a maximum of three attorneys assigned to Las Vegas at any one time.

Stanley Hunterton was one of those lawyers. Hunterton grew up in New York. After completing law school in 1975, he joined the Strike Force. He was initially assigned to the Detroit office; in 1978 he was sent to Las Vegas.

Things hadn't been going very well for the law in the time preceding Hunterton's arrival. Metro was reeling from the Joe

Blasko scandal, the FBI was recovering from allegations of agent misconduct, and Tony Spilotro was somehow beating back every attempt to put him out of business.

"A lack of confidence in Metro kept us from having an institutional association with them at the time. But we [Department of Justice lawyers] and the FBI were later able to develop several relationships with Metro personnel on a personal level," Hunterton recalls.

As Emmett Michaels, Stanley Hunterton, Charlie Parsons, Dennis Arnoldy, Lynn Ferrin, Joe Yablonsky, and their colleagues arrived in Las Vegas, they became united in their mission: rid Las Vegas of the influence of organized crime, including hidden mob ownership of the casinos, and the related financial crimes. Like their local law-enforcement brethren, the federal forces launched a vigorous campaign against the gangsters controlling and looting Sin City.

7

1979

As the 1970s neared an end, things heated up in the law's battle against Tony Spilotro. And Sheriff John McCarthy quickly learned that organized crime wasn't his only problem—far from it. But his new administration brought about quick and positive results in the relationship between Metro and the FBI.

FBI agent Emmett Michaels welcomed the improvement. In a 2004 interview, he recalled the night in 1978 that he and a team of agents bugged and wiretapped Spilotro's Gold Rush. "At that time Metro had a reputation of being corrupt, so we didn't tell them we were going to place bugs in Spilotro's store and tap the phones. There were about ten agents involved altogether. I and three other guys were up on the telephone poles when the alarm system activated. A Metro car showed up and the officer got out to investigate. The four of us dangled from those poles, holding our breath and hoping the cop didn't look up. He didn't. He left a few minutes later without detecting us." Had they been caught in the act, the incident would have been embarrassing at the least and word may have gotten back to Spilotro at the worst.

With attention from the McCarthy administration, the situation got better and information sharing resumed. For Sheriff McCarthy and Metro, this was an important step. Other problems needed to be confronted that year, however. Some were inherited and others were new.

Jail Woes

The problems in the Clark County Detention Facility first came to light in 1973 when a convicted murderer who was being temporarily housed in the facility filed allegations that conditions inside the jail constituted cruel and unusual punishment. A grand jury was convened to investigate the inmate's complaints.

In 1975, the grand jury found the charges were well-founded. They determined the lockup was overcrowded, understaffed, unsanitary, provided inadequate medical treatment, and was generally unsafe and dangerous to the health and lives of the inmates. Their report concluded that these conditions constituted an emergency situation and a new facility needed to be built. It sounded good, but nothing was actually done and the problems worsened.

In August 1977, inmates filed an amended complaint, stating that conditions were oppressive, barbaric, and degrading. They further alleged violations of their human and civil rights. The U.S. Justice Department joined the lawsuit on the side of the prisoners in February 1978. In July, the county entered into a Jail Consent Decree, establishing a committee to study all alternatives that would bring the detention system into compliance as soon as possible. Written recommendations had to be submitted by March 9, 1979, less than three months after McCarthy took office.

Gary Lang remembers the detention facility as being a hellhole in 1979. "There were continual water leaks from decaying lines and valves. Inmates frequently added to the problem by stopping up their sinks and toilets. The water would eventually seep through the floor and into the courtrooms located below."

Lang believes the jail issue was the result of many years of neglect by the politicians. "They had spent very little money on keeping the police up to speed with advancing technology or increasing personnel in a rapidly growing community. The philosophy was to provide the cops with just enough funding to keep the lid on. It was more beneficial to a politician's future to vote to spend money on a new park than a jail."

As part of his reform campaign, John McCarthy was determined to change the old way of doing business. Rather than play along with those controlling the purse strings, he challenged them. Attorney Lang described the relationship between his boss and the politicos as "combative."

Whatever the reasons leading to the jail crisis, the matter had to be resolved. At Lang's advice, McCarthy formed a task force to deal with and implement the Consent Decree requirements. Experts in jail administration were located and hired. New highly qualified architects were retained to replace the less experienced ones who had previously been employed through the political process. Progress lurched forward.

Gary Lang recalls one particular problem that he participated in resolving during the planning stage: the best way to move inmates from the site of the new jail to the courthouse, 480 feet away. Some decision-makers were pushing for a skyway running from the top floor of the lockup. Learning of the plan, Lang intervened. "I said that would be great—until the first time one of the prisoners pissed on a car or someone's head down below. The skyway was scrapped in favor of a tunnel system."

John McCarthy described addressing the Consent Decree as, "The most complex and demanding problem in the history of southern Nevada. If I'd had no other responsibility other than dealing with that one issue, my plate would have been overflowing."

He and his staff studied the Decree and identified 248 separate issues requiring correction. They included overcrowding, poor-quality food, meals served only twice per day, inadequate and dirty bedding, inadequate medical care, security, and recreational facilities, and lack of a law library. A chart was developed listing all 248 items and a target date for each to be corrected. That document was presented to a federal judge to show that Metro had a plan in place to bring the facility into compliance. It also placed some of the responsibility on other county officials.

Through repairs, renovations, and innovative release programs for certain felons and first-time offenders, McCarthy was able to keep the situation under control while a new jail was being built.

The corrections center was definitely a time-consuming headache for the new administration. But there was a second facility used to house inmates—the jail annex, located in the City Hall complex, and for two days that August, it took the administration's mind off the Consent Decree.

Takeover

The specifics of this incident are covered in detail in *Policing Las Vegas* and won't be repeated here. However, as a major event in Sheriff McCarthy's term, it deserves some mention.

On the morning of August 25, 1979, three inmates took control of the Jail Annex, located on the second floor of the Las Vegas City Hall complex on Stewart Avenue. A Hollywood screenwriter could have written the script for the incident. It had all the ingredients of an action movie: hardcore cons facing long sentences with little to lose; security equipment not working; procedures not followed; and escape within the grasp of the inmates, though they didn't know it. But it was not a staged event. It was very real, and before it was over people were dead.

The three convicts involved were Patrick McKenna, Felix Lorenzo, and Eugene Shaw. All were awaiting transfer to a state prison facility. McKenna and Lorenzo had recently been transferred to the Annex after having been implicated in a plot to start a riot at the Clark County Detention Center.

McKenna was a 33-year-old white male with a long history of problems with the law. An escape artist and convicted rapist, he was serving three life sentences plus 75 years for sexually assaulting two women in Las Vegas in 1978. He was also facing a murder charge for killing his cellmate while housed in the Clark County Detention Center.

Lorenzo, a Latino, was 30 years old at the time. He'd been sentenced to 160 years in prison for numerous armed robberies. He'd taken hostages during his capers, and on one occasion held an off-duty Metro officer captive for a short period of time. He was no stranger to prison strife, having been incarcerated at the Attica Correctional Facility in New York State during the infamous riot in 1971.

Shaw, a 41-year-old black male, was another convicted armed robber, doing a 60-year sentence.

In the aborted escape attempt, three correction officers were taken hostage. The ensuing standoff lasted nearly 48 hours. At its conclusion, Lorenzo and Shaw were dead as the result of a gun battle in which the three inmates engaged, and one correction officer was wounded in his hand by a stray bullet.

During talks between the convicts and police to end the standoff, Sheriff McCarthy decided to remain in his office and out of the way just yards from the Annex. "I had no special training in negotiating. Our negotiators were doing a great job and didn't need any interference from me. I made major decisions as necessary, but kept out of the direct negotiations," he explained.

Just as it seemed progress was being made toward a peaceful resolution, shooting broke out inside the jail. Confusion reigned. Sheriff McCarthy described his feelings this way: "To say it was the most dramatic incident of my law-enforcement career would probably be an understatement. My heart was in my throat when the shooting started. At the outset we didn't know for sure who was firing and why. Were the officers being held hostage the targets? Nobody knew. We didn't learn until later that it was an inmate-on-inmate situation and our tactical unit wasn't involved. There were some very tense minutes until things got sorted out."

The jail incident was the most dramatic event of the year for John McCarthy and the media coverage was mostly positive. The Sheriff, however, received his share of negative ink during that 12-month period.

Deconsolidation, Allegations, and Divorce

The Las Vegas City Council wasted little time in putting Sheriff McCarthy to the test. Legislators drafted a bill to deconsolidate Metro and create separate city and county police departments. The councilors claimed the move would provide the city with better protection at less cost. Metro and Clark County were vehemently opposed to the idea. This was an issue that popped up repeatedly during McCarthy's term and had to be beaten back each time. Even when the deconsolidation efforts were out of public view, they continued to simmer under the surface.

Then, ironically, the new Sheriff was forced to defend himself from reports in local newspapers claiming that organized crime was attempting to gain influence over him. One story alleged that Spilotro money had actually paid for McCarthy's post-election victory party. This was a real slap in the face to the man who had campaigned on the promise of ridding Las Vegas of the Ant and his ilk. McCarthy vehemently denied the allegations and they were never proved, but they were an omen of things to come.

While those controversies raged on, in October the local chapter of the NAACP accused Metro of mistreating blacks. They alleged that some cops operated under the premise that all blacks were criminals, or at least prone to crime, and weren't entitled to the same rights afforded other citizens. Sheriff McCarthy responded, admitting that misconduct could sometimes occur in a department with 900 sworn personnel. He argued that any mistreatment of blacks involved disrespect and not physical abuse. One officer was already under investigation for misconduct and other cases were pending, he assured them. McCarthy also used the charges as an opportunity to reach out to the black community, asking that a dialogue be established to make sure similar complaints were handled fairly.

Also in October, Kent Clifford and the Intelligence Bureau found their way into the media limelight in a negative way. Two local gun-shop owners, who had been arrested for criminal possession of brass knuckles, questioned the tactics used by Clifford's detectives during the investigation that led to their arrests. After making their complaint, the pair claimed they received anonymous threatening phone calls. A female police informant they knew supposedly told them that the cops were planning to retaliate against them. It wouldn't be the last time Commander Clifford and his officers would be accused of using questionable methods.

October 1979 ended with the newspapers reporting that McCarthy had filed to divorce his wife of nearly 22 years, from whom he had long been estranged. He was remarried to Sandra Greene in 1980.

On the organized-crime front, two incidents occurred during the year that later had a major impact on the law's altercation with Tony Spilotro.

Frank Cullotta

In early 1979 a new player was added to the Spilotro team. Frank Cullotta, a Chicago native and boyhood pal of the Ant, arrived in Las Vegas. Cullotta didn't just show up out of the blue. He had an extensive criminal record and had recently been released from an Illinois prison. Tony had gone to Illinois, where he and some of the old gang threw Frank a coming-out party. At that celebration, Tony extended an invitation for the 41-year-old ex-con to join him in Vegas. Cullotta accepted the offer and was soon enjoying life in Sin City as one of Spilotro's trusted lieutenants.

An accomplished burglar, Cullotta oversaw the operation of the Hole in the Wall Gang. However, thievery wasn't his only forte. He was also capable of violence and carried out killings when ordered.

The Lisner Murder

At approximately 4:30 a.m. on October 11, 1979, a dead man was found floating face down in the swimming pool of his residence at 2302 Rawhide Avenue in Las Vegas. He'd been shot in the head several times by a small-caliber handgun. The deceased was 46-year-old Sherwin "Jerry" Lisner. His wife Jeannie, a cocktail waitress at the Aladdin, found the body. She'd left work early after becoming concerned when her husband failed to answer her telephone calls and made the grisly discovery.

According to investigating police officers, Lisner had put up quite a fight. Bullet holes were discovered throughout the inside of the dwelling and blood was found on the walls and floor leading from the garage, through the residence, and out to the pool. Although the house had been ransacked, the cops didn't believe robbery or burglary was the motive. They declined to speculate on the reason Lisner was killed, but they did have a theory on how the murder went down.

The killer, or killers, knocked on the garage door, surprising Lisner. When he answered the knock, the shooting started. Although wounded, the victim attempted to escape his assailant, running through his home, the would-be killer in close pursuit and bullets flying. After a valiant effort to survive, Lisner's luck ran out when he reached the pool. No murder weapon was found and no suspect named.

But the police had their suspicions on the why and who of it. They knew that the dead man had mob connections. He'd been arrested by the FBI on July 11 and charged with interstate transportation of stolen property, aiding and abetting, grand larceny, and conspiracy. Free on $75,000 bail, Lisner was scheduled to go on trial October 29, in U.S. District Court in Washington, D.C.

Lisner was also known to have been acquainted with Tony Spilotro, though he wasn't considered to have been a member of the Ant's crew. He'd been rumored to be a part-time informant for the Drug Enforcement Agency and was believed to have been negotiating with the FBI to work out a deal in the cases pending against him in Washington. Those particular charges had no direct ties to Spilotro or the Outfit, but Tony was aware the feds wanted him bad. If they got Lisner talking, what guarantee was there that the conversation wouldn't include Tony and his Las Vegas activities?

Metro investigators knew all this and drew the logical conclusion that in Spilotro's mind, Lisner had to be considered a threat. And, as everyone was learning, people in that position tended to meet violent ends. So the police had a pretty good idea that Tony was behind the Lisner murder, but they couldn't prove it at the moment. A couple of years later their suspicions bore fruit. Frank Cullotta admitted that he was the triggerman in the killing of Jerry Lisner.

In *Of Rats and Men*, author John L. Smith explains the Lisner murder this way. Spilotro, growing increasingly paranoid under law-enforcement pressure, decided not to take any chances with the potential snitch. He assigned Frank Cullotta to do the hit. The killer in turn tapped Hole in the Wall Gang member Wayne Matecki to assist him. The pair drove to Lisner's house on the night of October 10. Cullotta went to the door while Matecki remained in the car monitoring a police scanner. When his target answered the door, Cullotta talked his way inside and when Lisner turned his back, shot him twice in the head.

The situation turned a bit surreal at that point, as Smith quotes Cullotta. "He turns around and looks at me and says, 'What are you doing?' Then he takes off running through the kitchen toward the garage.

"I actually look at the gun like, what the fuck have I got, blanks in here? I take off after him and empty the rest into his head."

Cullotta eventually accomplished his task, but only after Matecki had to bring him additional ammunition. In all, he shot Lisner 10 times before dragging the body outside and dumping it in the pool. Jerry Lisner was dead, but his murder subsequently played a major role in the downfall of the man who had ordered his execution: Tony Spilotro.

8

1980

The first year of the new decade saw continuing growth in Las Vegas Valley. The population reached 461,826, and 12 million tourists dropped in. *New York, New York* by Frank Sinatra made it to the number-two spot on the pop-music charts. It was also an eventful year for Sheriff McCarthy, and for Tony Spilotro and his pursuers.

In January, the local newspapers reported that the homicide rate in Clark County had reached a record high and the overall crime rate was also on the rise. These statistics provided fodder for McCarthy's critics, who were watching his performance with a sharp eye.

In February, the news hit that the Sheriff's son had been arrested for selling narcotics to an undercover officer. To his credit, McCarthy had advance knowledge of the investigation and made no attempt to interfere. Still, it was a difficult time for the county's top lawman.

"I had received information from field officers that my oldest son, Michael, had been observed in the vicinity of dope dens and in the company of dope dealers," McCarthy remembers. "I sent word back to the officers that Michael was to receive no special treatment. If he was in the wrong, they should arrest him because he knew better.

"Michael and his brother had the same upbringing, attended the same schools, and had mostly the same teachers. Brian worked his way through college, graduate school, and law school. Today, he's a successful attorney licensed to practice in Nevada, California, and Arizona. Michael's life took almost an opposite road. I'll go to my grave never understanding why the drug problem happened."

Right on the heels of the disclosure about his son, Sheriff McCarthy sustained another blow. A judge ruled that the law creating the Las Vegas Metropolitan Police Department was unconstitutional. The proponents of deconsolidation had won a major victory, dampened only by the judge's decision to stay the dissolution of the department until McCarthy could appeal to the Nevada Supreme Court.

Calling the ruling "a severe blow to the concept of Metro," the Sheriff vowed to fight for the survival of his agency. In addition to battling in the courts, he appealed to the public to mobilize on his side. The fate of Metro would remain unresolved for more than a year. The uncertainty placed additional strain on McCarthy and all the department's employees, both sworn and civilian.

But the police weren't the only ones under stress. Around that same time, Lefty Rosenthal's worst fears came true: The affair between his wife and Tony Spilotro became public.

Blowup

As time went by, both Geri and Tony had become increasingly careless about keeping their adultery under wraps.

"Spilotro openly flaunted his relationship with Geri as a show of power. He could have had dozens of women, younger and prettier. It was a stupid thing to do," Kent Clifford said.

For Geri's part, early in the year she began appearing in

her favorite haunts all decked out in a mink coat and diamond ring that generated ooohs and ahhhs from her cronies. She wasn't shy about divulging the source of the adornments: Tony Spilotro.

The word was out. It had to be embarrassing for Lefty, but he chose to ignore rather than confront the situation. It was a strategy that worked for several months, until everything came to a head.

It was September 8. Geri Rosenthal had been out all night. When she got home at around 9 a.m., she was high on drugs, booze, or both. Finding herself locked out of the house, she became enraged. Getting back into her Mercedes, she repeatedly rammed her car into the rear of Lefty's parked Cadillac. There was damage to each vehicle, but they both remained drivable. The commotion brought Lefty out to his front porch and a number of neighbors onto their lawns. A security guard called the police.

At the sight of her husband, Geri exited her car and took up a position on the lawn, shouting at him. She said the FBI wanted to talk with her and she just might go see them. She also announced that Tony Spilotro was her "sponsor" (protector) and wanted to know what Lefty planned to do about it.

During her tirade a police car pulled up and the officers tried using their verbal skills to calm down the out-of-control woman. Soon after the police got there, another car arrived. Nancy Spilotro was the driver.

"As I remember that morning, Lefty called me and said that Geri was outside the house raising hell. He asked if I'd come over and see if I could help," Nancy Spilotro said in a 2004 interview. "I went right over. I was still in my pajamas, covered by a robe."

While the police continued trying to reason with Geri, she pulled a pearl-handled revolver from under her clothing and waved it in the general direction of her husband. The police officers dove for cover behind their car. Neighbors scurried for safety. Lefty remained where he was, seemingly unable to move. That was when the five-foot 97-pound Nancy Spilotro sprang into action. She launched herself at the other woman.

"I must have been quite a sight, flying through the air in my pajamas and robe," she laughed. Funny or not, the diminutive Spilotro was effective. She wrestled the larger woman to the ground and disarmed her. With the danger over and additional police cars on the scene, the spectators returned to their positions to watch the rest of the action.

Geri decided this was an appropriate time to make her move. She told the police she wanted to go into the house to get some personal items, and then she'd leave. An officer escorted her while Lefty was made to wait outside. The keys to the safe deposit box were among the things Geri collected while inside. When she was finished, she told the officers she had to go to the bank to take care of some business and she didn't want her husband to interfere. The police said they'd accompany her and make sure she was able to do her banking undisturbed.

It was an odd convoy that headed toward the bank. Geri was in the lead, the police behind her, and Lefty bringing up the rear. Both of the Rosenthal vehicles looked like they were survivors from a demolition derby.

Upon arriving at the bank, Geri went inside and emptied the safe deposit box of an estimated $200,000 in cash and $1 million in jewelry. An increasingly frustrated Lefty was held at bay outside.

According to the police report of the incident, after leaving the bank, "Mrs. Rosenthal jumped back into her car and took off at a fairly high rate of speed," in the direction of California.

Shortly afterward, Geri's father received a phone call from Tony Spilotro at his home in California. "You know a lot, but you don't know anything. Understand?" the gangster said. The message apparently had its desired effect. Subsequent attempts by the FBI and Metro to interview Geri were rebuffed.

Three days later, on September 11, Lefty filed for divorce. When it was finalized the following January, he was awarded custody of the children and ordered to pay Geri $5,000 per month in alimony.

Although there may have been some moments of humor involved, the highly publicized event didn't generate any laughter from Tony's bosses in Chicago.

Turmoil at Metro

A bombshell story authored by reporter Paul Price appeared in the *Las Vegas Sun* on April 3. Two veteran lawmen believed they were under surveillance and investigation by Metro. One of the alleged victims was Beecher Avants. The former Metro detective had resigned when McCarthy was elected and taken a job as Chief Investigator with the Clark County District Attorney's Office. The second man was none other than Undersheriff John Moran. Sheriff McCarthy, who reportedly had sanctioned the investigations, declined immediate comment. The article did point out that both men were potential candidates to oppose the Sheriff in the 1982 election.

"I was shocked when I read that story," John McCarthy said in 2004. "There had been a strained relationship between Moran and me since I won the election. I think he saw himself as the eventual successor to Ralph Lamb and my election screwed things up. I tried to assuage those feelings by giving him an active role in decision-making. But he never seemed to take an active interest.

"Prior to that article I thought we had been making some progress in smoothing things over. We had been getting together for dinners along with our wives and it seemed to me we were getting on the right track. After reading the Price story, I felt like I had been stabbed in the back. My first thought was why? If he really thought those things were true, why didn't he confront me? I think I could have proved the allegations weren't factual."

To back up his argument, McCarthy insisted that the surveillance and investigation described in the article would have taken a team of four or five officers unknown to the subject. The story named one detective, whom Moran knew personally. That officer would have been called in and confronted with the allegations. A private meeting would also have provided a chance for Moran to present any other evidence he had and given the Sheriff an opportunity to respond. Going directly to the press and making the matter public took that option off the table, of course.

"I called him [Moran] into my office when I got to work that morning and asked him those questions. He said he'd heard about the alleged investigation from some of his closest friends on Metro, but declined to name them. I told him I'd deal with the issue at a later time and ended the meeting."

After Moran left, the Sheriff continued to ponder the incident. He came to the conclusion that some of the quotes in the piece attributed to Moran didn't reflect the way his accuser normally expressed himself. McCarthy became convinced the whole thing was a hatchet job and that Moran had not acted on his own. In fact, he suspected that the *Las Vegas Sun* itself had made some sort of deal with Moran, possibly offering its support in the future election in return for his collaboration. There was no love lost between McCarthy and *Sun* owner Hank Greenspun, and the Sheriff believed the newspaper had a "get-McCarthy" attitude.

But Moran and Avants weren't the only ones to allege the Sheriff was up to no good. "Several other politicos joined the hue and cry, claiming I was having them followed, too. They included Clark County Commissioners Manny Cortez and Jack Petitti, State Senator Floyd Lamb [Ralph Lamb's brother], Las Vegas City Councilman Ron Lurie, and Harry

Claiborne, a federal judge," McCarthy said.

The *Las Vegas Review-Journal* ran a story the same day as the Paul Price article in which it was alleged that McCarthy was compiling an "enemies list" consisting of his political opponents. Commissioner Manny Cortez was quoted as saying Metro insiders had told him that he'd been under investigation for six months and some "compromising" information had been developed.

At a press conference the following day, McCarthy denied all the charges. He announced that he planned unspecified disciplinary action against John Moran for misconduct in taking his grievances directly to the media. Four days later Moran was fired; he vowed to fight his termination.

Politically, Sheriff McCarthy was at odds with some of the most powerful and influential people in Las Vegas and Clark County. These were differences that would never be reconciled.

As promised, John Moran took his case to court and in early June won a decision ordering him to be reinstated with all back pay and benefits on June 17. He returned to work, but announced his resignation just over a week later, saying he and McCarthy "will never get together on anything."

Many of the political insiders saw Moran's resignation as paving the way for him to challenge McCarthy in the next election.

On June 5, a page-two headline in *The Valley Times* read, "Metro Police Battle Erupts At City Hall." The story cited a resolution calling for the city to keep the concept of Metro. The document was supposedly developed in a meeting between the mayor, a county commissioner, and Sheriff McCarthy. The city representatives were enraged for two reasons, saying the resolution was the equivalent of dropping their lawsuit to dissolve Metro, and because they hadn't been included in the meeting at which the resolution was generated. The future of Metro remained in doubt.

Surveillance by Metro

Keeping an eye on the bad guys could often be boring work. If the cops weren't concerned about being detected, they'd sometimes play mind games with their subjects. One of their favorites was to aim the laser sight of their rifle on one of the bad guy's chests as they stood around talking outside a bar or restaurant. Until the targets realized what was going on, their reactions when the red dot of the laser was noticed centered over someone's heart were often comical. Thinking the dot was a stain on their shirt or jacket, they tried to wipe it away. Eventually, they figured it out, then become angry, or sometimes scared. If they spotted the location of the surveillance car, obscene gestures and expletives would be directed toward the detectives, and were sometimes returned by the laughing lawmen.

Another tactic was for the detectives actually to enter the restaurant or bar where their subjects were and get as close to them as possible. In general, the targets didn't appreciate the unwanted company. Some of them ignored the cops, while others became confrontational. In cases where they were ignored, the cops sometimes initiated a dialogue with the gangsters. Their comments were usually derogatory or mocking, and often prompted a response. Many times these encounters ended in pushing and shoving matches, with one or more of the bad guys shedding their coats and preparing to duke it out. The officers would defend themselves if necessary, but usually they just laughed in the faces of their challengers and walked out. Encounters such as these kept the pressure on Tony and his boys.

There were also, of course, covert operations, some of which weren't completely successful. A former detective related an incident in which a tracking device was planted on a mobster's car. "The guy we were tailing pulled into a restaurant and went inside, presumably to have dinner. We waited a few minutes and then my partner crawled under his car to attach the device. He no sooner got under there than the guy leaves the restaurant and gets back in his car. I figured he'd either run over my partner when he pulled out or at least spot him if he checked his rearview mirror when he drove away. To this day I don't know what he was doing, but he sat in the car for a few minutes, then got out and went back into the restaurant. My partner finished up and everything was okay.

"The next morning we're following the guy and he pulls in a service station for an oil change. As soon as the mechanic got the car up on the hoist he spotted the damn thing and told the subject about it. The guy got his lawyer and they went downtown and complained about police harassment. Sometimes *we* got lucky, and other times *they* did."

Two of Kent Clifford's officers, Detective David Groover and Sgt. Gene Smith, decided to take advantage of Spilotro's use of police scanners to have a little fun with him. Knowing the Spilotros were hosting Tony's birthday party, they parked about a half block from the Ant's house. Using a frequency they knew Tony monitored, Smith made a radio transmission to Groover, making it seem as though they were in separate vehicles. Passing the microphone back and forth, the two cops carried on a conversation. Smith asked if Groover had the papers that were to be served on Spilotro. Groover said he did, and that he and some other officers were on their way to Spilotro's home. Smith replied that he'd start heading that way and meet them there. Within minutes, Tony's guests, including Joe Blasko, Herb Blitzstein, and Frank Cullotta, along with Tony and Nancy, vacated the residence. Tony had to do his celebrating elsewhere.

A few weeks later David Groover and Gene Smith had another encounter regarding the Spilotro investigation. This time it wasn't a laughing matter. It was deadly.

The Maitre D'

On the evening of June 9, Groover and Smith were conducting another routine surveillance of the Spilotro gang. On that night they were camped outside the Upper Crust pizza parlor and the adjoining My Place bar, located at Flamingo Road and Maryland Parkway. Tony's pal Frank Cullotta had a financial interest in both establishments and they had become hangouts for the mobsters. Spilotro, Cullotta, and some of their associates were inside the Upper Crust, but nothing exciting was going on. For the two veteran cops, it had all the makings of another uneventful shift.

"We put in a lot of long tedious hours watching those guys. But in that kind of work things could change very quickly, and that night they did," David Groover said in 2003.

The changes began when a 1979 Lincoln with Illinois license plates pulled into a parking space in front of the Upper Crust. Spilotro, Cullotta, and another associate were now sitting at a table outside the restaurant. The operator of the vehicle went inside the eatery, apparently to order a pizza to go, then came back out and joined Spilotro and the others at the table. They talked for several minutes until the new guy's pizza was ready. At that point he got back in the Lincoln and drove away. The detectives weren't sure who this new player was, but it was obvious that he was acquainted with Tony. Smith and Groover decided to follow the Lincoln to see what information they could gather about who he was and what he was up to.

"As soon as he pulled out onto Flamingo, he started speeding, doing eighty or better, and driving recklessly. I was driving our unmarked car and Gene was in the passenger seat," Groover remembered.

"Eventually, we figured we had enough probable cause on the traffic violations to pull the car over and check out the driver. By that time we were on McLeod near a new housing development called Sunrise Villas and the Lincoln had slowed to the speed limit. I put the red light on the dash and activated it for the guy to pull over. The Lincoln turned onto Engresso, the street running into the development, went past an unmanned security booth, and stopped several yards beyond. I parked behind him, got out of the car, and approached the Lincoln, verbally identifying myself as a police officer and displaying my badge. As I neared the other car, it pulled away at slow speed, stopping again a short distance away. I got back in our car and followed, angling the police car in and again getting out and approaching the Lincoln. This time Gene got out and took up a position by our passenger door."

At that time, Groover and Smith didn't know that the Lincoln was being driven by Frank Bluestein, a 35-year-old maitre d' at the Hacienda Hotel & Casino, one of the properties controlled by the Chicago Outfit. Also known as Frank Blue, Bluestein and his girlfriend lived in Sunrise Villas. His father, Steve Bluestein, was an official in the local Culinary Union and had been the subject of a 1978 search warrant as part of the FBI investigation of Tony Spilotro.

"This time as I neared the Lincoln, the driver lowered his window. I again identified myself and displayed my badge. Suddenly Gene hollered, 'Watch out, Dave! He's got a gun.' I returned to our car and took up a position behind the driver's door. Gene and I continued to yell at the guy that we were cops and to put down his gun. He never said a word, but instead of getting rid of the weapon, he turned slightly in his seat, opened his door, and started to get out of the car. The gun was still in his hand and aimed toward Gene. Believing the guy was about to shoot, Gene and I opened fire."

At approximately 11:45 p.m., shots rang out. Several rounds struck Bluestein. He was rushed to a nearby hospital, where he died a couple of hours later. A .22 handgun was recovered at the scene. But as far as the Bluestein family, Tony Spilotro, and Oscar Goodman were concerned, this was not a justified use of deadly force. It was a police execution, with the cops planting a gun on their victim to add legitimacy to their actions.

It was a time that Dave Groover will never forget. "There was a real firestorm over the Bluestein shooting. We were accused of murdering the guy, planting a gun, and all that stuff. We ran a check on the gun Bluestein had and traced it to his brother, Ronald. The gun had been purchased in Chicago. That pretty much blew the planted-gun charge out of the water. We didn't release that information right away, though. We waited until the coroner's inquest to make it public."

Less than two weeks later, a coroner's jury ruled the death of Frank Bluestein to be a case of justifiable homicide. The cops were okay in that regard, but the verdict didn't prevent the filing of numerous civil suits against them. One was a $22 million whopper accusing the cops of violating Bluestein's civil rights. All of the cases were eventually decided in favor of the police, but the civil-rights suit dragged on for five long years.

As the civil actions were being filed, Groover and Smith knew they had acted appropriately and were confident they would prevail in the end. Other than the annoyance of dealing with the lawsuits, they weren't overly concerned. But they learned a few months later that whatever was being done to them by the Bluestein family's attorneys was the least of their worries.

Upper Crust

Metro wasn't the only law-enforcement agency interested in the Upper Crust pizza parlor. The FBI also knew that Tony and his colleagues frequented the restaurant. And when the gangsters went into a back room there, it was logical to assume it wasn't to discuss the weather. Agents wanted to know exactly what was being talked about in private. They made their case to a federal judge, who issued an order to bug the eatery. It wasn't easy.

"The place was in the middle of a strip mall, with legitimate businesses on either side. They were open around the clock, besides. We ended up going across the roof and installed a camera and microphone down an airshaft. It was very ticklish and time-consuming, but we got it done without being detected," Emmett Michaels said.

That was the good news. The bad news was that an Upper Crust employee discovered the bugs less than 24 hours later. He informed Frank Cullotta, who in turn summoned Tony Spilotro. The camera and microphone were ripped out and all transmissions ceased.

Soon afterward, agents Charlie Parsons, Emmett Michaels, and Michael Glass met at their office to figure out what to do next. "We came to the conclusion that the camera and microphone were government property and had been legally installed. We decided to go to the Upper Crust and get our equipment back," Charlie Parsons said, recalling the incident.

When the agents arrived at the restaurant, they found Cullotta and Spilotro in no mood to cooperate. Emmett Michaels warned Spilotro that he'd better surrender the FBI's property or there would be trouble. Tony attempted to contact Oscar Goodman, but the lawyer was out of town. A second attorney, Dominic Gentile, was reached and responded to the restaurant. Gentile directed his client to comply and the camera and microphone were returned without incident.

According to Charlie Parsons, that confrontation laid the groundwork for future events. "Getting the property back wasn't the real story. The most important thing that happened that night was that Frank Cullotta saw Tony try to back us down and fail. Tony intimidated a lot of people and he tried that crap with us. I know Cullotta was impressed that we stuck to our guns and walked out of that place with what we came for."

Another Lawsuit

On August 5, just weeks after Frank Bluestein was killed, Oscar Goodman launched an attack directly on Sheriff McCarthy and Metro for allegedly harassing Tony Spilotro and his associates. In a class-action lawsuit, Goodman asked the court to restrain John McCarthy from continuing a program of harassment that had been ongoing since November 2, 1979.

In a related article in the *Las Vegas Sun* on August 5, Goodman is quoted as saying, "I believe the lawsuit will protect the citizens of the state of Nevada from false arrests, harassment, and possibly injury or death that has taken place in the past." Goodman charged that Bluestein's death was the direct result of police harassment. He added of the alleged police conduct, "I think it's un-American. These are really Gestapo-like tactics. It literally has become a police state in this community."

In the lawsuit, the lawyer said, "The object and purpose of this program is to make unlawful any unfounded investigatory detentions and arrests of Spilotro and any persons observed in his company or known to be an associate of Spilotro."

In addition to McCarthy, the suit named nine Metro intelligence officers, including Kent Clifford, and 20 unnamed officers as defendants.

The *Sun* article went on to report the specific charges leveled by Goodman. He said that since November 1979, the police had kept Spilotro and nearly a dozen of his friends under intensive surveillance, stopped and interrogated Spilotro and his friends without lawful or reasonable ground under the false guise of making some police investigative inquiry, and made false accusations or alleged minor traffic violations as a pretext for jailing persons known to be associated with Spilotro.

Attacking the Sheriff directly, Goodman said, "[McCarthy] didn't care whose rights were being violated. He said it was legitimate police work."

The attorney said the killing of Bluestein was the "last straw" in leading to the filing of the lawsuit. In Goodman's opinion, Metro officers had conducted a high-speed chase of Bluestein, who had committed no violations of the law, and gunned him down while carrying out Metro's harassment policy against Spilotro.

Goodman and the Ant were clearly on the offensive.

McCarthy Fires Back

On the same day, Sheriff McCarthy issued a press release in response to the lawsuit and Goodman's comments. The release read:

"It appears that we have struck a nerve in organized crime in this community.

"When high-priced criminal lawyers attempt to restrain this department from enforcing the law against their clients, this sets the tone for less affluent criminals to take note of these exceptions and conclude that they should also be exempted to prey on this community.

"Criminals and organized crime figures operate behind closed doors and at night to avoid the scrutiny of law enforcement. These legal maneuvers are merely a ploy.

"Our interpretation of the U.S. Constitution extends to everyone the right to be secure from the hoodlum element, and I for one am sick and tired of the courts in this country preserving the rights of the criminals at the expense of the public.

"It's really a pity that Mr. Goodman has gone to the extreme to make his point in his pleadings by dragging out the Bluestein shooting again. This matter was settled by a coroner's inquest that determined the shooting was in self-defense, and that the deceased was armed with a weapon that had been in his possession for several days before the shooting took place. This shows me that Mr. Goodman's scruples are in question here.

"Mr. Goodman also asks for damages in behalf of Mr. Spilotro. I say let the self-respecting citizens of this county sue Mr. Spilotro for the black eye he has given us and run him out of town."

Sheriff McCarthy's statement was printed in the *Review-Journal* the next day, and the media war was on.

Sniping

In the days that followed, Oscar Goodman and Sheriff McCarthy engaged in verbal battle by way of the news media. The *Sun* and *Review-Journal* found that the combatants were rock-solid in defending their positions and neither was reserved when it came to making comments to the press.

In response to the Sheriff's press release, the attorney claimed that McCarthy had a "Neanderthal" attitude toward Tony Spilotro. "He should be running for Grand Imperial Wizard of the Ku Klux Klan," Goodman suggested. "Wherever I go the people are expressing phenomenal support for my position. They believe that Sheriff McCarthy's statement was so juvenile."

He offered McCarthy some advice on how he should be doing his job. "Instead of engaging in personalities, he had better spend his time apprehending murderers, rapists, robbers, and kidnappers who are running loose on the streets of Las Vegas."

Goodman also expressed puzzlement over the amount of attention the law was giving to Tony Spilotro. "It's incredible to me that Mr. Spilotro is subject to so much criticism, when the only arrest for which he has ever been convicted was to help someone fill out a bank application for which he received a $1 fee. The Sheriff must be hallucinating, because I'm sure if Mr. Spilotro were committing any crimes, the Sheriff would arrest him. And he hasn't done that."

McCarthy quickly answered, alleging that some of the statements Goodman had made to the press constituted violations of Nevada Supreme Court rules. He quoted from

Rule 199. "A member of the bar should try his cases in court, not in the news media. No statement should be made which indicates intended proof, or what witnesses will be called, or which amount to comments or arguments on the merits of the case."

Wasting no time, Goodman again attacked McCarthy and his press release. "He advocated getting a lynch mob and running my client out of town. I find that an irresponsible statement for a public official to make."

Judge Troubles

Within two weeks of the lawsuit being filed, three judges were disqualified in an unquestioned basis or after admitting they had opinions on the case. The fourth judge assigned to the case announced he was disqualifying himself, after being asked to bow out by the District Attorney's Office because he had previously expressed concerns about police making traffic stops in unmarked cars. The matter had to be returned to the clerk for the random selection of yet another judge. By the time an acceptable judge was found, eight of the 12 District Court judges had either been disqualified, or disqualified themselves, from presiding.

Oscar Out?

In September, the District Attorney's Office acted on Sheriff McCarthy's charges that Oscar Goodman had violated Supreme Court rule 199 in regard to his statements to the press. The D.A. filed a motion to have Goodman and his law firm disqualified from the harassment case for misconduct and unethical behavior. The brief filed in support of the motion alleged that Goodman's comments had "prejudiced the defendants' [McCarthy and his officers'] rights and have cast this judicial district and this case in a poor public light."

The lawsuit was dismissed when Tony Spilotro refused to give a pre-trial deposition. In *Of Rats and Men*, Oscar Goodman explains the end of the case this way. "Eventually, they wanted to take his deposition, knowing he wasn't going to let them. I couldn't prevent them from taking Tony's deposition. Tony never said boo to law enforcement, so I wasn't about to expose him and the case was dismissed."

The Foul Fowl and Other Tales

While Sheriff McCarthy's dealings with politicians were often contentious, there were some humorous moments, too. For example, during a September meeting of the Las Vegas Metro Police Commission, McCarthy accused the commissioners of acting like a gaggle of geese. The next day a messenger, with a group of reporters in tow, delivered a package to McCarthy aide Norm Ziola.

"It was a fifteen-pound goose," Ziola recalled with a chuckle in 2004. "It was from Commissioner Paul Christensen and had a note that said, 'So you will be able to tell the difference, this is a goose.' We all had a laugh and the reporters took a lot of pictures. I was wearing a brand new sports coat that day and while we were posing for the photos, the damn goose crapped all over it."

McCarthy named the department's new mascot "Paul."

Gene Smith recounted having to make a confession regarding some booze missing from McCarthy's office. "McCarthy had a television in his office and kept a supply of Scotch inside a big world globe. It happened I had pass keys for most of the offices, including his. We were on the afternoon shift and a popular cop show was running at the time. ... I think it was 'Hill Street Blues.' Anyway, on the night the program was on, I'd take my squad into McCarthy's office and watch it on his television. I considered them training sessions. On occasion we'd have a swig or two of Scotch while watching TV.

"Eventually, McCarthy noticed his Scotch inventory wasn't what it should be. He was none too happy about it and figured that our custodian was the culprit. When I found out the janitor was going to be confronted and possibly disciplined, I had no choice but to confess. I got off pretty easy, but our TV nights were over."

Smith also remembered a courtroom encounter with Oscar Goodman he found amusing. "Frank Cullotta was in court for a residential burglary and Oscar was representing him. I was on the stand in civilian clothes being cross-examined. Goodman noticed that I was armed and raised that as an issue with the judge. He said he didn't feel safe having an armed witness. The judge said that police officers were welcome to be armed in his court, including while on the stand.

"We broke for lunch and when I came back I had a package with me. As soon as I got back on the stand, Oscar asked me what was in the package. I opened it and pulled out a bulletproof vest. I told him I thought he might want to put it on so he'd feel safer about me having a weapon. Oscar went ballistic and demanded the judge do something. The judge said, 'When you asked what was inside the package you opened the door for his answer. Now let's move on.' I don't know as Oscar thought it was funny, but there were a lot of chuckles in that courtroom."

Former McCarthy insiders cited a couple of other incidents that can be laughed at now, but weren't particularly funny to them at the time. The first case involved a local newspaper reporter whose articles tended to be critical of McCarthy and his administration.

"This particular reporter was very negative toward us and frequently wrote hit pieces based on rumor and anonymous sources. I went to him and asked that he check with me before writing stories that reflected poorly on the department. I promised I'd be honest with him and if we'd screwed up, I'd admit it. But if the allegations weren't true, I wanted a chance to refute them before they hit the paper. He agreed and our relationship improved for the next several weeks," McCarthy's former assistant said.

"Then one morning before leaving for work, I grabbed the paper off my porch and found it contained a scathing article about Metro. Surprised and disappointed, I stopped in to see the reporter on my way to the office. I asked why he hadn't given me a chance to state Metro's side of the story before he ran with it. His response was that he'd been at an event at the Riviera a couple of days earlier and Sheriff McCarthy had also been in attendance. The reporter was in the men's room when he noticed McCarthy was at the next urinal. He said hello. John replied, 'Fuck you,' and walked out. Our truce was over and the reporter went back into the attack mode."

In another incident, a senior staff member recalled working for several weeks to set up a meeting between Sheriff Mc-Carthy and a couple of City Council members with whom he was feuding. Finally, the session was scheduled to be held in the restaurant at the top of the Mint.

"When everyone showed up, I excused myself and went to another table so the meeting would have an element of privacy. Before I had a chance to order a drink, I heard Mc-Carthy say, 'Go fuck yourselves.' He then went storming out toward the elevators. I caught up with him and asked what had happened. He said, 'They told me that if we worked together we could control Las Vegas and the entire county. I ran for office to change how these people have been doing things, not to join them.'

The maverick McCarthy had done what he thought was right. But needless to say, the encounter did little to mend any fences.

Frank Cullotta Arrested

On November 20, Metro Intelligence Bureau officers arrested Frank Cullotta on charges of possession of stolen property. While executing a search warrant at Cullotta's residence on that date, the police found property listed on an earlier burglary report. Cullotta and a female companion refused to provide an explanation regarding how the goods came into their hands. They were both arrested and taken to jail.

This was far from Cullotta's last trip to the lockup.

Gotcha

Also in November, it appeared that the Ant had finally made a mistake that could land him in the local slammer. He was reportedly observed having breakfast in one of the casinos, a violation for Tony and others who'd been black-booked. A security guard at the Sahara called Metro and reported that the FBI had brought the crime-in-progress to his attention. A detective was dispatched to the Sahara and arrested Spilotro, who was unable to provide any identification. The subject was whisked away to jail.

Gene Smith got word of the arrest and went to the booking area to check things out. In a matter of seconds, he realized there'd been a mistake. "The detective they sent to the Sahara wasn't part of the Spilotro investigation and wasn't all that familiar with Tony. He'd arrested a Spilotro all right, but it wasn't Tony. I told him to cut the guy loose immediately." The cops had taken Patrick Spilotro into custody. A dentist from Chicago, he was Tony's brother, with a strong physical resemblance. Patrick had every right to be in any casino he chose to patronize.

Kent Clifford and his men knew that Metro had been the victim of a setup. The alleged FBI tip had been a fake. The flap was seized upon by the Spilotros to further their claims of harassment. The print news media had a story of police incompetence that would bring a lot of chuckles and head-shaking from their readers—all at Metro's expense.

There was little doubt that Tony Spilotro was laughing the hardest of all.

Death at the MGM

At 7:20 a.m. on November 21, a non-Spilotro event occurred that bears mentioning because of the loss of life involved and its effect on the safety standards imposed on every hotel in Las Vegas: The MGM broke out in flames. If sprinkler systems had been required at the time, the fire would likely have resulted in relatively minor property damage. But they weren't, so the ground-floor kitchen where the blaze started was dangerously vulnerable to fire. Before the inferno was brought under control, 85 unfortunate souls perished. A Metro helicopter crew consisting of pilot Sgt. Harry Christopher and Officer Tom Mildren became heroes that day for evacuating panicked guests and employees trapped on the roof of the 26-story building.

The tragedy resulted in new safety codes that make the hotels in Las Vegas among the safest of any tourist city in the country.

9

1981

The courts are the legal mechanism for people seeking to redress perceived wrongs. The courts were used to go after the police in the Bluestein shooting case. But after the cops were cleared of any criminal wrongdoing by the coroner's inquest, some people apparently didn't feel that the pending civil actions would provide the justice they sought. In late February, Metro was informed by the FBI's Chicago office that they'd picked up credible information about contracts put out on the lives of David Groover and Gene Smith. The two Intelligence Bureau officers were marked for death and two hit men from Chicago were on their way to do the job. After stopping in Denver to obtain a clean weapon, the would-be cop killers would soon be in Las Vegas.

The mob tries to best the police by corrupting them or outsmarting them, not by killing them. People who prefer to stay below the law's radar screen rarely order the murders of two cops. It brings down too much heat. The news caught Metro by surprise.

Kent Clifford remembers when he first heard about the contracts. "For quite a while after the Bluestein shooting, there had been a verbal battle in the press between the department and the Bluestein family's lawyers. There had also been several civil cases filed, and I thought that's all that was going on. Then we get word that Groover and Smith are going to be killed.

"I went berserk. Spilotro knew my goal was to put him in prison for the rest of his life; I'd told him that more than once. We were adversaries, but there were certain rules we played by. You didn't put contracts out on cops. And even if Tony didn't actually order the hits, he damn sure knew about them. Nothing like that was done in Las Vegas without Spilotro's knowledge and approval."

As upsetting as the news was, Smith and Groover may not have been the sole intended victims of the Chicagoans.

Were There Three?

The FBI wasn't the only source of information Metro received regarding hit men being in town. Former Clark County Deputy District Attorney Jim Erbeck, who subsequently successfully prosecuted Frank Cullotta and convicted other members of the Hole in the Wall Gang, along with several other organized-crime figures, believes he may also have been a target. He received information from a friend, whom he considered a highly reliable source, that he was of interest to men from the Windy City. Mr. Erbeck recalled the incident during a 2005 interview.

"At that time I had been with the DA's office for just about a year and had previously volunteered to prosecute organized-crime cases. There was a bar and restaurant called T.K. Christy's located at 300 Las Vegas Boulevard South, across from the federal and county courthouses. It was one of the favorite watering holes for politicians, prosecutors, FBI agents, and cops. I stopped in regularly as it was handy to where I parked my car while at work.

"I remember going into Christy's one night after the

Bluestein shooting and hearing some very disturbing information. One of the female employees I was acquainted with told me that three men had been in asking questions about me and two Metro detectives. She knew one of the men from her previous job. He was from Chicago and was 'connected.' The other two were strangers to her. They asked her things like how often I stopped in, where I parked my car, and if I knew or hung around with certain Metro detectives. She told them that I was a customer and she knew me. But she also said she didn't keep track of my movements or social circles and couldn't be much help to them. The encounter had shaken her up. She was scared to the point that she wouldn't give me a description of the men.

"I immediately called Metro Intelligence and reported what I'd been told. They asked me to go about my normal activities, including frequenting Christy's. I was to park in my usual place in the parking garage. Metro said they would have the area under surveillance and attempt to determine if I was being watched or followed, and by whom.

"After a few days I was advised by Metro that two men were keeping an eye on me and that they had been identified as hit men from Chicago. A short time after that, I was notified that the situation had been resolved and there would be no further problems."

Regardless of the number of intended victims, Clifford, Groover, and Smith believed then, and they believe now, that the hit men were acting on behalf of the Bluesteins.

"I moved my family out of state for their protection," Gene Smith recalls. "Cops were assigned to stay at my house. We were waiting for those guys when they hit town and checked in at the Fremont Hotel downtown. They were under surveillance around the clock. One of the people they met with was Ron Bluestein, Frank's brother. The supposed hit men were in Vegas for about a week, but only came near my place once. They stopped a couple of blocks away, then left the area. I don't know what happened; maybe they got cold feet. We eventually confronted them and had a little chat. They headed back to Chicago shortly afterward."

In a further effort to build a case against the Bluesteins, after the hit men arrived in town, an application was made to wiretap the phone of Steve Bluestein. The tap was approved, but only after an altercation with Clark County District Attorney, Bob Miller.

"The DA didn't like to use wiretaps," Kent Clifford recalls. "When we met to discuss the matter, he asked me why I didn't like him. I said it wasn't that I didn't like him. It was that I had raw intelligence information that he was associating with one of the people who had organized the skim from the casinos. The DA said the guy was an old friend and that there was nothing the matter with them socializing. I argued that in his position as DA, he shouldn't have that kind of a relationship with an organized-crime figure. He said I could think what I wanted, but the association would continue.

"While the wiretap was running, we made reports to the judge who had issued the warrant. On the second day of the tap, he told me that a high-ranking member of the DA's office had called him and asked that the tap be shut down. After our conversation, the judge refused the request. The next day a piece appeared in the *Las Vegas Sun* stating that an informant had told them about the Bluestein wiretap. When that article appeared, Bluestein's phone went dead. Besides Metro, the only other people who were aware of the tap were the DA's office and the judge."

Ned Day Weighs In

Gene Smith and Dave Groover hadn't been intimidated by the death threats and proved it a few days later. The following piece by reporter Ned Day, writing for *The Valley Times*, appeared on March 18:

"You had to be there. But believe me, it was a classic.

"Picture the My Place cocktail lounge (Tony Spilotro's favorite hangout) about 11 p.m. last Friday night. Just a few of the boys bending their elbows and trading war stories.

"Then, the door opens and in walks six feet and 230 pounds worth of Metro Intelligence cop Gene Smith, who grabs a corner barstool and nonchalantly orders a drink.

"Smith, you may remember, is the cop who trailed Frank Bluestein from a meeting with Spilotro outside My Place, a trail that ended in a hail of gunfire with Bluestein very dead.

"In case the My Place crowd didn't instantly recognize him, Smith grandly introduced himself to the bartender in a stage whisper loud enough to be heard the length of the bar.

"Smith and his partner then just sat in the corner, smiling sweetly and sipping on drinks for about 20 minutes.

"I mean, talk about showing the colors in enemy territory. That's like sending a PT boat up the Volga River. You have to admit, the guy's got flair."

Gene Smith remembers the incident. "There was one thing left out of that story. While we were there Tony Spilotro bought us a drink. I took the two glasses over to Tony and told him we were pretty damn particular about who we drank with or accepted drinks from. Then I told him what he could do with his drinks."

Not long after that, Smith received a picture mailed to him anonymously. The photo was of Tony Spilotro accompanied by attorney Neil Bellar. It contained a caption that read, "To Gene, Thanks for everything, you rotten bastard." It was signed "The Ant." The picture generated a lot of laughs around Smith's unit, but he doubts it was actually sent by Spilotro. It was likely a prank by one of his detectives.

The immediate threat was over, but would someone else show up to make an attempt on the lives of the detectives? In Kent Clifford's mind, the only way to remove the danger once and for all was to have the contracts lifted. He was also quite sure that Spilotro had authorized the hits on his own and his bosses in Chicago weren't aware of them, but there was only one way to find out for certain. In an unprecedented move, Clifford decided that he needed to go to Chicago and have a face-to-face with Tony's superiors.

Trip to the Windy City

Clifford took his plan to Sheriff McCarthy, who agreed that he and another detective could make the trip. Distrusting the DA's office, they decided not to consult with them or inform them of the pending visit. The department would pick up the tab for the plane fare; the officers had to pay for their own accommodations. He next called the FBI in Chicago and obtained the home addresses of Joe Aiuppa, Tony Accardo, and Joseph Lombardo. It was time to head east.

In March, Clifford and his previous partner, Galen Kester, boarded a plane for Chicago. The people they planned to talk with were violent individuals and meeting with them could prove dangerous. Both Clifford and Kester carried handguns in their briefcases in the event things didn't go well. The cops checked into a motel and were on the road in a rental car early the next morning. Their first stop was at the home of Joseph "Doves" Aiuppa, current head of the Chicago Outfit. Kent Clifford recalls that eventful and sometimes frustrating day.

"Aiuppa wasn't home when we arrived; only his wife was there and she wouldn't let us in. I told her it was very important that I talk with her husband. I left her the phone number for our motel and asked her to make sure he called me.

"Our next visit was to the home of Joseph 'Joey the Clown' Lombardo. He wasn't home either, but his wife invited us into the house and we talked for about ten minutes. We left the same message with her as with Mrs. Aiuppa. From there we stopped at Tony Accardo's, but he was out, too. Three stops and three misses."

Not ready to give up, Clifford remembered a man from Chicago who had visited Spilotro in Las Vegas and was known to be mob-connected. He contacted the local FBI office and obtained the office address for Allen Dorfman.

Dorfman ran a business as an insurance broker, but his real forte was in obtaining Teamster Pension Fund money to finance the Outfit's Las Vegas interests. He'd been tried along with Jimmy Hoffa in 1964 for diverting pension-fund money for their personal use. Dorfman was acquitted, but Hoffa was found guilty. The broker was convicted in 1971 of accepting a $55,000 kickback to arrange a Teamster loan and spent nine months in prison. Not long after getting out of stir, he was a co-defendant with Tony Spilotro and Joe Lombardo on another pension-fund-related fraud charge. All three got off the hook when the government's chief witness against them was murdered.

"When we got to Dorfman's office I walked past the reception desk looking for him. The secretary said I couldn't do that and I told her to watch me. I guess it was quite an entrance," Clifford continued. "Anyway, we got to see Dorfman and explained the situation to him. He said to go back to the motel and someone would be in touch.

"That afternoon a lawyer representing the mobsters called. I ran the whole scenario by him and requested a personal meeting with his clients. He said he'd talk with them and get back to me. He called back awhile later and said there would be a meeting that evening, but I wasn't invited. Although that didn't make me very happy, there wasn't a lot I could do about it. I told the lawyer to relay a message to his clients just like I gave it to him. I said, 'If you kill my cops I'll bring forty men back here and kill everything that moves, walks, or crawls around all the houses I visited today. And that is not a threat, but a promise.' The lawyer said he'd deliver my message exactly as I gave it. If the contracts were lifted, he said I'd get a phone message saying, 'Have a safe journey home, Commander.' If I didn't get a call, it meant all bets were off.

"I dozed off and around 2 a.m. the phone rang. A voice I couldn't identify told me to have a safe trip home. The contracts were lifted."

As for Allen Dorfman, the insurance broker and conduit for illegal loans was gunned down in a gangland-style murder in January 1983.

Shotguns Roar

Kent Clifford returned from Chicago believing the war against Tony Spilotro would again be fought within the acceptable guidelines. A sense of normalcy did return, but only for a few weeks. At around 10 p.m. on April 9, someone launched a shotgun attack on the home and vehicle of Tony Spilotro and the nearby house of his brother John. Fortunately, no one was hurt during the shooting, but both houses and their parked vehicles were damaged. At 10:47 p.m., John Spilotro reported the incident to the police. The subsequent investigation failed to identify the assailants.

In August, John Spilotro contacted Bob Miller, Clark County District Attorney, and demanded an investigation. He told a *Las Vegas Sun* reporter that he went to the DA, because the police had failed to do a thorough investigation and that he believed the shooters had actually been cops. He alleged that the shotguns had been in the hands of Gene Smith and Detective Bob Gillispie. Spilotro said that not only had his property been damaged, the shotgun blasts had placed him and his family in great personal peril, with some pellets narrowly missing the heads of his two sons. The police motive was supposedly the continuing policy of harassment that had been initiated by Sheriff McCarthy and Kent Clifford.

The *Sun* also reported that a secret witness had come forward claiming to have observed Gene Smith in the act of loading a shotgun in the vicinity of the Spilotro homes the night of the shootings. The witness had allegedly identified Smith from a photo lineup.

Metro denied its officers were involved, stating that records showed Smith and Gillispie were two miles away from the Spilotro neighborhood at the time of the incident, and were being interviewed by a Metro patrol officer regarding a traffic accident their unmarked car had been involved in.

The DA entered into the case, launching an investigation into the shotgun blasts. That started a three-way war that was fought in the press. Metro Undersheriff Don Denison suggested that by stepping into the case, Miller had placed himself in the position of having to "either call for arrest warrants or grand jury indictments, or give the two officers an apology."

Miller shot back, "I don't owe an apology to the police department for doing my job. I'm doing what I was elected to do."

Metro officials then contended that Miller's decision to get involved had been the result of pressure by Spilotro's attorney, Oscar Goodman. The DA flatly denied that allegation. "I haven't talked to Oscar Goodman for months," he said.

Meanwhile, the Spilotro side continued to express the opinion that the Bluestein shooting and the shotgun incidents were related events in an ongoing police plot. The shotgunning was a message sent by the cops to intimidate them.

After a six-week investigation, the DA declared that there was insufficient evidence to warrant charges against the police. Miller explained, "To the very best of our abilities, based on all the evidence presented, the two Las Vegas Metropolitan Police officers cannot be held responsible for the shotgun incident." He declined to provide specifics about the evidence, except to say that the witness who supposedly saw Gene Smith loading a shotgun failed to identify the officer from a photo lineup.

Smith scoffs at the story told by the alleged witness. "He

said I was near a convenience store when he saw me. What in the hell would I be doing out there with an empty shotgun? His story didn't make any sense."

According to Smith, if the shootings were meant as a message to the Spilotros, the lawmen weren't the authors. "That happened right after Kent Clifford went to Chicago and blew the whistle on Tony. Maybe his bosses were getting fed up with him and wanted to get his attention."

The additional violence and war of words didn't sit well with Kent Clifford. Having had enough, he called Oscar Goodman and asked to have a meeting with the Spilotro brothers. The session was held soon afterward in the lawyer's office with the Spilotros, Goodman, and Clifford present.

As the four men took seats around Goodman's desk, Clifford sensed that the meeting was being taped. He suggested that they move to a couch and chairs about 10 feet away. The Spilotros agreed, but Goodman said no, they should stay where they were. That convinced Clifford they were being recorded. On the record or not, the conversation got pretty heated. Clifford remembers the dialogue this way:

"Commander, you went to Chicago and told them you have forty men. I have four hundred men," Tony Spilotro snarled.

"That makes us even, doesn't it?"

Spilotro stared at the cop questioningly for a few seconds. "How do you figure?"

"My people are Vietnam combat veterans, and they're each worth ten of your street punks," Clifford explained.

"I next told him that my men hadn't done the shooting at John's or his place and that we were not out to kill him or anybody else. He accused me of making a statement on TV that I intended to kill him. He was talking about something I told a reporter after the incident at the Sahara where we mistakenly arrested his brother Patrick. I said then that there would be another day. To a guy like Tony, that indicated a death threat, because that's the way his mind worked. I clarified that my statement meant that I intended to put him in jail for the rest of his life. That would be better justice than killing him. When I left that meeting, it was understood that the personal stuff was over and things would be back to normal."

Arrests

While all that was going on, Metro continued its efforts to put pressure on Tony Spilotro and his boys. Ernest Davino, one of the Hole in the Wall Gang regulars, was arrested on January 22. During a search of his residence at 2:45 that morning, a lock pick and a vial containing 26 black and orange pills were discovered; the pills were determined to be illegal drugs. Davino was charged with possession of burglary tools and possession of a controlled substance. Out on bail, he was arrested again on October 15, pursuant to a grand-jury indictment charging him with burglary and possession of stolen property.

On May 26, Lawrence Neumann—burglar, robber, and convicted killer—was observed seated in a parked vehicle in the vicinity of the Upper Crust. Interviewed by detectives, they determined that Neumann was an ex-felon who had failed to register with the police department upon his arrival in Las Vegas. After Neumann was taken into custody on that charge, his car was searched. Found in the glove box was a .380 Mauser semi-automatic pistol. A check of the weapon revealed it had been stolen in a burglary on April 9. As a result, Neumann was additionally charged with receiving stolen property and as an ex-felon in possession of a concealed weapon.

On July 28, police investigating a burglary-in-progress call at an auto-parts store located near the Upper Crust nabbed Leo Guardino. Guardino attempted to flee the area in his car, but was apprehended by the officers. He was arrested again in October pursuant to a grand-jury indictment charging him with burglary and possession of stolen property. The cops didn't have to chase Guardino to arrest him this time; he was already in jail on yet another burglary charge.

All three of these men, and a few of their associates, were busted on another burglary-related charge during the year. But that caper had repercussions that would rock the world of organized crime.

Deconsolidation Attempt Fails

The issue of dissolving Metro was still unsettled. In April, a special three-member state Senate panel held a hearing in Carson City to attempt to resolve the matter. In often heated debate, Las Vegas officials proposed that a Chief of Police position be created to run Metro effective January 1983. That would have relegated Sheriff McCarthy to the relatively minor role of running the jail and serving civil papers. Metro and Clark County were spirited in their opposition. McCarthy argued that the top law-enforcement officer in the county should be someone elected by the voters, not a political appointee.

The panel subsequently submitted recommendations that were incorporated in a bill intended to clean up the 1973 law that had created Metro and was later ruled unconstitutional. The city's argument to change the leadership of Metro failed and wasn't included in the panel's suggestions. But the city politicians vowed to fight on.

A few weeks later, the same representatives who'd been at each other's throats for months met again in Carson City. This time the atmosphere was much friendlier after reaching a compromise that more of Metro's funding would be shouldered by Clark County. The shift amounted to an additional burden of $4 million for county taxpayers and an equal savings for Las Vegas residents. In return, the city dropped its effort to have a Chief of Police oversee Metro. The department was saved, and John McCarthy wouldn't have to confront the matter again.

Challenge

Sheriff McCarthy had very little time to celebrate his victory over the deconsolidation proponents before another headache emerged. John Moran told a *Las Vegas Sun* reporter that although he hadn't officially declared his candidacy, he was organizing a campaign to run against McCarthy in the next election. Moran said he had a lot of workers already on board and they were passing the word that he intended to be in the race.

That announcement must have made the news media salivate. A race between John McCarthy and John Moran had the ingredients to generate a lot of ink. The former number-two man in the department would be trying to unseat the man who had once fired him. They apparently weren't very fond of each other and neither man was likely to back down if things got nasty. In fact, they'd be more apt to counterattack. For those interested in local politics, the entire scenario promised to be exciting.

Bertha's

It was the Fourth of July and it was hot. It was always hot in Las Vegas in July, but to many of the 40 or so FBI agents and Metro officers working a special assignment, it seemed even hotter than normal. And that was only the temperature. If things worked out as planned, the heat would get even more intense for Spilotro's Hole in the Wall Gang.

The center of the law's focus that day was Bertha's Gifts & Home Furnishings, located at 896 East Sahara. The store was in an upscale single-story building and included a jewelry shop on the premises. The lawmen believed a burglary was scheduled to take place there in the evening, with the thieves expecting a take of around $1 million in cash and jewelry. That kind of haul was a big score, especially in 1981 money, and the HITWG crew assembled to carry out the burglary reflected that. Criminal stars Frank Cullotta, Wayne Matecki, the homicidal Larry Neumann, Leo Guardino, Ernie Davino, and former cop Joe Blasko were poised to hit Bertha's.

Their opposition was headed on-scene by the FBI's Charlie Parsons and Joe Gersky and Metro's Gene Smith, now a lieutenant. Their bosses—Joe Yablonsky and Kent Clifford—were nearby, available if needed to make any necessary command decisions.

Although the actual crime wouldn't take place until after dark, the lawmen were at work much earlier in the day. After weeks of preparation, the final plans had to be made and a command post and necessary equipment needed to be set up. Surveillance teams were active around Bertha's all day, monitoring activity and making sure they were thoroughly familiar with the area. They had to keep an eye on the bad guys as well, looking for any indication of a change in their plans or other potential problems.

With two different agencies participating in the operation, communications were particularly important. Their radios had to have a common frequency, but one that wasn't known to the burglars. A secret frequency was obtained and divulged only to those with a need to know. At the same time they continued to use the regular frequencies, those likely to be monitored by the thieves, to disseminate bogus information as to the location and status of personnel. In the late afternoon, the balance of the agents and officers deployed to the field.

The main observation point to observe the roof of Bertha's was from the top of a nearby five-story building. Charlie Parsons and Joe Gersky took up positions there, along with the equipment and personnel to videotape the scene. Gene Smith worked with the surveillance detail, riding with an FBI agent. The burglars were not to be arrested until they actually entered the building, making it a burglary rather than the lesser charge of an attempted crime.

The cops believed that at least four vehicles would be used

by the crooks, three of them to conduct counter-surveillance activities and one to transport the three men who would go on the roof and do the break-in. Frank Cullotta, driving a 1981 Buick, Larry Neumann in a late-model Cadillac, and an unknown individual—possibly Joe Blasko—in a white commercial van with the name of a cleaning business and a "Superman" logo on the side would represent the gang's forces on the ground. The occupants of all three vehicles would be equipped with two-way radios and police scanners. The burglars, Matecki, Guardino, and Davino, would arrive by station wagon and go on the roof to gain entry to the store. They would also have radios to keep in contact with the lookouts on the ground.

At around 7 p.m., the HITWG counter-surveillance units began to appear. Cullotta and Neumann repeatedly drove around the area, apparently checking for a police presence or anything that seemed suspicious. In turn, they were being tailed by cops and agents. The white van took up a position in the driveway to the Commercial Center shopping plaza, across the street from Bertha's. From this vantage point, the operator—believed to be Joe Blasko—had an unimpeded view of the store. As the man in the van watched, he was under constant surveillance himself.

While this game of cat-and-mouse continued, the whole operation almost came to an abrupt end. Gene Smith and the FBI agent were stopped at a traffic light when a car pulled up next to them. Out of the corner of his eye, Smith saw the driver of the other car was none other than Frank Cullotta. The cop—very well known to Cullotta—went to the floor of the vehicle as fast as he could. The light changed and Cullotta pulled away. It's almost a certainty that had Smith been spotted in the area, the burglars would have scrubbed their plans.

At approximately 9 p.m., a station wagon bearing Matecki, Guardino, and Davino arrived and parked behind a Chinese restaurant located at 1000 East Sahara. A police surveillance vehicle was parked nearby, but went unnoticed by the burglars.

The three men exited their vehicle and unloaded tools and equipment, including a ladder. They next proceeded to the east side of Bertha's and gained access to the roof, hauling their gear up with them.

From the roof a few buildings away, the videotape was rolling. The burglars were obviously unaware they were walking into an ambush. Plugging into electric outlets located in the air-conditioning units, they went about their business, using power and hand tools to penetrate the store's roof. Everything was going smoothly for both sides. Other than Lt. Smith's close call with Cullotta, the only thing that had gone wrong for the law so far was that a member of one of the surveillance teams had to be treated for dehydration.

Agent Dennis Arnoldy was in charge of a four-man team, two FBI and two Metro, responsible for arresting the thieves on the roof. They relaxed as best they could in the back of a pickup truck in the parking lot of the Sahara Hotel & Casino, located a few blocks from Bertha's.

Arnoldy and his team weren't expecting their prey or the lookouts to be armed. These were veteran criminals. They knew that if they were caught with guns, the charges against them would be more serious and the potential penalties would be greatly increased. The lawmen certainly hoped that would be the case and that the arrests would be made without bloodshed.

As the burglars progressed in their efforts to get through the roof, Arnoldy and his men made their way to the scene. Using a ladder, they got onto the roof. An impressive fireworks display exploded in the sky over Las Vegas as the lawmen secreted themselves behind vents and air-conditioning units to wait for the pre-determined arrest signal to be broadcast. At that point a minor snag developed when the burglars broke through, only to realize they hadn't hit their target: the store's safe. Recovering quickly, they soon made another entry in the right place. At approximately 10:40 p.m., Leo Guardino dropped through the opening and into the store, carrying the tools necessary to break into the safe. The act of burglary was then complete.

Arnoldy, shotgun at the ready, heard a broadcast over his radio that he thought was the arrest signal. But due to the noise from the constantly running air conditioners, he couldn't be sure. He hesitated for just a few seconds, then directed his team into action. When Davino and Matecki detected the lawmen approaching they scurried to the front of the building and possible escape. But when they looked down on Sahara, they saw a number of agents and officers on the sidewalk below them pointing weapons in their direction. Knowing the game was up, they surrendered without incident. A few seconds later Guardino's head popped up through the hole in the roof and he was taken into custody.

At street level, other agents and cops were already busy apprehending the lookouts. Neumann and Cullotta were nabbed a short distance from Bertha's. Agent Gary Magnesen and two Metro officers arrested Joe Blasko. In a 2004 interview, Magnesen recalled the incident.

"One of the Metro officers was in uniform and driving a black and white. Our plan was for the marked car to come up on the van from the rear with its lights flashing and headlights illuminating the van's interior. Another detective, armed with a shotgun, and I with a pistol approached the van from the front and ordered the occupant out. Up until that point we thought it was Blasko inside, but we weren't positive. In fact, some of the cops didn't want to believe that their former colleague had really gone to the dark side. When Blasko got out, the cop recognized him and said, 'Son of a bitch.' This was the best joint operation I was part of while in the Bureau."

No weapons were found on Blasko or any of the other arrestees.

When agents and officers entered the store, they found that the gang's second hole in the roof had been accurate, located directly over the safe. Burglary tools were found nearby and several holes had been drilled into the safe in an effort to open it. Leo Guardino had been a busy man during his short time inside the building.

Joe Yablonsky and Kent Clifford held a press conference shortly after the arrests were made. They told reporters that Frank Cullotta, age 43, Joe Blasko, age 45, Leo Guardino, age 47, and Ernest Davino, age 34, all of Las Vegas, were in custody. Also arrested were Lawrence Neumann, age 53, of McHenry, Illinois, and Wayne Matecki, age 30, of Northridge, Illinois. The six men were charged with burglary, conspiracy to commit burglary, attempted grand larceny, and possession of burglary tools. They were all lodged in the Clark County Jail.

When reporters asked how the lawmen happened to be in the area at the time of the burglary, Yablonsky and Clifford weren't very specific. They denied that the arrests were the result of an informant's tip. But they did admit being aware that Bertha's was scheduled to be hit on the Fourth of July. The story the reporters were given that night wasn't exactly true, though. And there had really been seven gang members present at Bertha's, not six.

What the reporters weren't told was that Sal Romano, an expert at disabling alarm systems, was working as a part of the HITWG's counter-surveillance team that night. Unbeknownst to the rest of the crew, two agents from the FBI's Tucson office, Donn Sickles and Bill Christensen, had flipped Romano several months earlier. Based on information he provided, the lawmen knew virtually every detail of the gang's plan well before July 4. When the signal was broadcast to arrest the burglars, Romano was immediately removed from the area and placed in the Witness Protection Program. His role in the Bertha's operation wasn't made public until several years later.

But the Outfit knew there had been a traitor and they didn't like it. It wasn't Romano individually; it was that he,

Weasel Fratiano, and others were becoming snitches. A pattern seemed to be developing that made Chicago nervous. Once-trusted members and associates were making deals to save their own skins. Honor among thieves seemed to be rapidly becoming a thing of the past.

Prostitution

Sheriff McCarthy was making good on his promise to fight organized crime. Other issues, however, were giving him real headaches. One major problem that came to the forefront in late 1981 was the world's oldest profession. Prostitution was illegal in Clark County.

The Valley Times ran an article on November 3 stating that the situation was so bad that tourists were unable to walk the Strip without being confronted by working girls. There had been 15,000 prostitution-related arrests so far in the year, with a scant 48 convictions. The girls tended to be aggressive and didn't like to take no for an answer. They sometimes physically grabbed onto a male and tried to take him along with them. If he had a female companion with him, she'd be invited to either come and watch or join the action.

Sheriff McCarthy responded that he not only had insufficient personnel to mount the foot patrols necessary to deal with the problem, but that the laws were inadequate. The District Attorney said he couldn't do much with bad arrests and weak cases. The judges argued that they were only able to impose sentences based on the laws currently on the books. Whatever the reasons, more aggressive enforcement was demanded. And that responsibility fell to Metro.

Although the public generally supported McCarthy's efforts to combat organized crime, people seemed more concerned about prostitutes than the thieves and killers of the Spilotro gang. Why?

In the opinion of one retired detective, most of the violence related to Spilotro was gangster-on-gangster and didn't have a visible impact on the average citizen, some of whom even found that the mob's presence added intrigue and excitement to Las Vegas. Spilotro's burglars targeted businesses or wealthy residents and tourists for the most part, again not involving a large segment of the overall population. But when a situation became more personal, attitudes changed; when a resident couldn't take his visiting uncle on a tour of the Strip without being propositioned, well, that was just too much.

The former cop compared the public attitude toward organized crime to that of a farmer who has a rat-eating snake in his barn. "He may not like snakes, but as long as the reptile doesn't pose a threat to him or his family and it helps to control the vermin population, he's willing to let it go about its business."

The prostitution problem became a major campaign issue the following year.

Cullotta Jailed Again

Frank Cullotta had been released from jail on bail following his arrest for the Bertha's burglary. But in November he was back in the slammer for a previous caper. In this case, a woman's home had been burglarized and her furniture stolen. The missing items were subsequently found in Cullotta's residence. He was indicted for possession of stolen property. Due to already being free on bond from the Bertha's arrest, the judge set a high bail. But the resourceful Cullotta was able to come up with the assets necessary to extricate himself from the crowbar hotel.

Spilotro's Days Are Numbered

To close out the year for Sheriff McCarthy, his son Michael—already on probation for a drug conviction—was arrested for driving under the influence of alcohol or drugs following a traffic accident on Flamingo Road.

Meanwhile, events occurring in 1982 proved to be the turning point in the law's fight against Tony Spilotro and his street-crime activities.

Left—Bugsy Siegel opened the Flamingo Hotel & Casino in 1946. This was the first Strip resort financed primarily with mob money (courtesy of UNLV Special Collections).

Below—Moe Dalitz (center) with Barbara Schick and Lee Majors 1979 (courtesy of UNLV Special Collections)

Above—Meeting of the Chicago Outfit, circa 1970s. From left to right (front row)—Anthony "Joe Batters" Accardo, Joseph "Black Joe" Amato, Joseph "Little Caesar" DiVarco, James "Turk" Torello; (back row)—Joseph "Doves" Aiuppa, Martin Accardo, Vincent Solano, Alfred Pilotto, Jackie Cerone, Joseph "The Clown" Lombardo (courtesy of Gene Smith).

Right—Allen Glick, President of ARGENT Corp. which owned the mob-controlled Stardust and Fremont Hotel and Casinos, circa 1978 (courtesy of UNLV Special Collections).

Left—Tony Spilotro with his criminal defense attorney Oscar Goodman (courtesy of Gene Smith).

Below—The "Frank Rosenthal Show," from left to right: Judy Angela, Lefty Rosenthal, Kim Cornell, Lucia and Barbara Beverly. Donn Arden is in front. The women were all dancers in the Stardust Lido show (courtesy of UNLV Special Collections).

Left—Sheriff John McCarthy (courtesy of John McCarthy).

Below—John McCarthy was sworn in by Judge Paul Goldmann, 1979 (courtesy of John McCarthy).

Bottom—Sheriff John McCarthy inspects recruits, 1979 (courtesy of John McCarthy).

Top—Bertha's Gifts & Home Furnishings, 896 East Sahara, 1981 (courtesy of Dennis N. Griffin).

Left—Herb Blitzstein, Tony Spilotro's trusted lieutenant (courtesy of LVMPD).

Above—2004 prison photo of Lawerence Neumann (courtesy of Illinois Dept. of Corrections).

Left—Bertha's burglars, July 4, 1981. From left to right: Ernest Davino, Lawrence Neumann, Wayne Matecki, Leo Guardino, Joe Blasko, and Frank Cullotta (courtesy of Gene Smith).

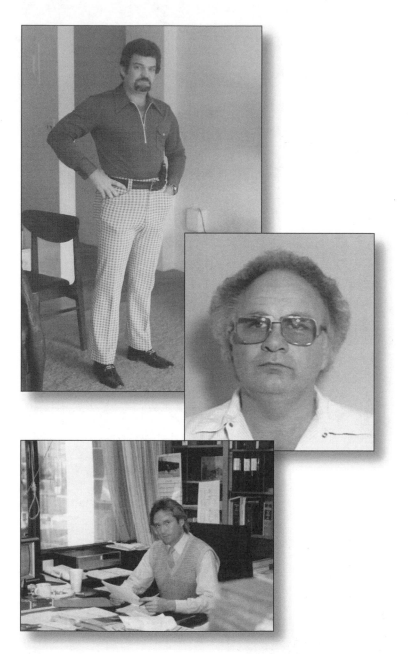

Top—Sgt. Gene Smith of the LVMPD, circa 1975 (courtesy of Gene Smith).
Center—Spilotro's associate Frank Cullotta (courtesy of LVMPD).
Bottom—Clark County DA and Organized Crime Prosecutor Jim Erbeck (courtesy of Jim Erbeck).

Clockwise from top left—FBI Agents Dennis Arnoldy, Lynn Ferrin, Gary Magnesen, Charlie Parsons, and Emmet Michaels (all courtesy of subjects).

Left—Gene Smith received this auto-
graphed photo of Tony Spilotro anonymously (courtesy of Gene Smith).

Below—Tony Spilotro and Oscar Goodman, April 1, 1980 (courtesy of UNLV
Special Collections).

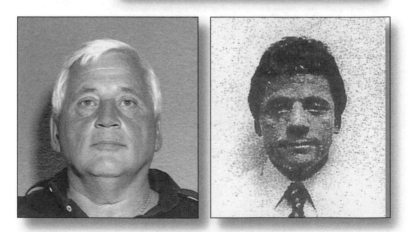

Above—Tony Spilotro's brothers. John Spilotro, left, moved to Las Vegas and
assisted in operating the Gold Rush. Michael Spilotro, right, resided in Chicago
and had criminal affiliations there. He was murdered with Tony in June 1986.
(courtesy of LVMPD).

Left—Lefty Rosenthal's car after getting bombed outside Tony Roma's restaurant (courtesy of Mike Bunker).

Left to right: Special Agent Mark Kaspar, Tony Spilotro, Special Agent Dennis Arnoldy, and Supervisory Special Agent Charlie Parsons (courtesy of *Las Vegas Review Journal*).

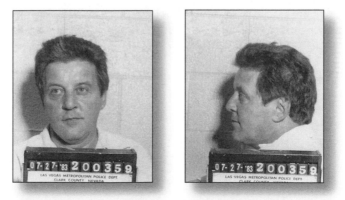

Above—Tony Spilotro's 1983 mug shots (courtesy of Gene Smith).

Left—Kent Clifford, Commander of the LVMPD Intelligence Bureau under Sheriff McCarthy (courtesy of Kent Clifford).

Below right—John Moran, Sheriff McCarthy's undersheriff and political nemesis (courtesy of LVMPD).

Below left—TV reporter and newspaper columnist Ned Day was Tony Spilotro's antagonist, circa late '70s (courtesy of UNLV Special Collections).

Tru Hawkins, life-long Las Vegan and host of the "Tru Hawkins Show" on KDWN Radio (courtesy of Tru Hawkins).

10

1982

The first quarter of the year began relatively calmly for Sheriff McCarthy, but things were brewing under the surface that would make for an exciting final eight months. An election battle loomed, which promised to turn nasty. There was more controversy involving the Intelligence Bureau and Commander Clifford's tactics. And there was a major breakthrough in the Spilotro investigation.

John Moran Announces

In early April, John Moran formally announced that he was tossing his hat into the ring to challenge his former boss for the county's top law-enforcement position. First though, he had to win in a primary contest against several other candidates.

Moran was 60 years old at the time and had been a cop in Las Vegas since 1948. He'd served as Chief of Police in the old Las Vegas Police Department from 1972 until the merger to form Metro in July 1973. As part of the consolidation agreement, Moran was installed as undersheriff to Ralph Lamb in the new department. Like John McCarthy, Moran was also a former Marine.

The apparent animosity between the two men, assuming both won their respective primaries, was bound to make for an entertaining election season.

Turning Point

On April 20, a jury convicted Frank Cullotta on the possession of stolen property charges from the previous November and he was sent back to jail. But this time, he faced the likelihood of being adjudicated a habitual criminal, for which he'd receive a possible sentence of life in prison.

Although his present incarceration had nothing to do with Bertha's, Cullotta knew he was in big trouble over that case. The prosecutors had him and his fellow burglars by the short hair and they were all looking at some serious prison time. But it was worse for Cullotta. He'd been in charge of the Bertha's gig and had bungled it badly. Why hadn't he detected Romano's treachery in time? Why hadn't the law's surveillance of Bertha's been spotted? Romano had turned rat; how reliable would Cullotta be if the law turned up the heat? Tony Spilotro and the Chicago bosses were no doubt asking those questions.

Metro also liked Cullotta for the 1979 Jerry Lisner murder and attempted to interview him about that killing while he was locked up. He'd rebuffed them so far, but he knew what they wanted to talk about. The cops didn't give up easily and kept the pressure on. And then the FBI arrived on the scene with new information that proved to be pivotal in the effort to attain Cullotta's cooperation.

Even though he was keeping Metro at bay, having been around crime and criminals for most of his life, Frank Cullotta could sense when all was not well in his world. The fact that Spilotro had violated mob protocol and wasn't taking care of him and his family spoke volumes. It was a bad sign indeed.

According to Gene Smith, "Frank and his girl had no money coming in and Tony wasn't looking out for him. Frank told me later that he placed calls to Tony from jail and Tony wouldn't come to the phone. Nancy would tell him that Tony wasn't home. Frank saw the writing on the wall."

Cullotta Rolls

On the afternoon of Friday April 30, FBI agent Charlie Parsons had a job to do before beginning his weekend. He contacted Cullotta's lawyer—who also represented other organized-crime figures—and asked to meet him and his client at the jail. Parsons left his office at around 5 p.m. and drove to the meeting. He explained to the two men that he had obtained credible information that the Chicago Outfit had authorized a contract to have Cullotta killed.

"We had a policy that if we were aware someone's life was in danger, we had to inform that person, regardless of who he was or what we thought of him," Parsons explained. "I told them that it had been a long week and that I would be brief. I made my announcement and left. The threat was real, but my matter-of-fact delivery was intentional, designed to get Cullotta thinking."

The strategy worked. Shortly after arriving at his office Monday morning, Parsons received a phone call. The caller said he was the man Parsons had talked with Friday afternoon. He wanted to meet again, this time without his lawyer.

For Tony Spilotro, things were about to start unraveling.

Frank Cullotta wanted to live, and preferably as a free man. In return for that chance, he was willing to talk. In just a few days, he had a new lawyer—one without mob connections—and an agreement with local and federal prosecutors. He would admit to various charges and serve a federal prison sentence determined by a judge and based on a recommendation from prosecutors. Any local charges that were not part of the plea arrangement would be dropped. After doing his time—which turned out to be eight years—he, his wife, and their daughter would be placed in the Witness Protection Program. To get that deal, Cullotta had to cooperate fully and honestly with law enforcement and testify in court proceedings as necessary.

Less than two weeks after Charlie Parsons had informed him of the contract on his life, Frank Cullotta was out of jail and his family was under law-enforcement protection. Still technically in the custody of Clark County, he was housed in various hotel and motel rooms around Las Vegas. For security purposes, the longest stay in any one place was two nights. Debriefing, which began immediately, was a joint effort by Metro and the FBI from the start.

"We worked hand in hand with the FBI," Gene Smith said. "Frank remained in our custody for about a month before we formally turned him over to the feds. Metro was responsible for his security during that stage and we knew the bad guys wanted him dead. I told my men, tongue in cheek, that if Cullotta got killed, there had better be a number of dead cops around his body to keep it company."

In addition to hotel rooms, Cullotta spent some of his time as Metro's guest in a well-equipped motorhome the cops had obtained during a drug bust. "Frank liked to fish and we took him out to Lake Mead for a couple of days so he could do some fishing. He really enjoyed that," Gene Smith recalled.

The lawmen treated Cullotta with respect and a bond soon developed between them. "He called me Lieutenant Gene," Smith said. "He came to think of himself as part of the team. I remember he'd say to me in his Chicago accent, 'We're gonna get these guys, ain't we?'

During the Metro phase of his debriefing, Cullotta provided information that allowed the police to clear about 50 of their previously unsolved burglaries. He also admitted to the Lisner killing. But in order to get a murder conviction in

Nevada, the law required that other evidence be presented to corroborate the suspect's confession. In the Lisner case, no such hard evidence could be found.

"We tried," Gene Smith said. "Frank took us out to where he said he threw away the murder weapon, but the gun wasn't there. It had been almost three years, though, so that didn't come as a big surprise."

As the FBI case agent, Dennis Arnoldy worked the Cullotta debriefing with Metro from the start. He remained Cullotta's primary interrogator after the feds took custody of the informant. "Once we took control of Frank, we got him out of Las Vegas. After that we only brought him back for legal proceedings. For Frank's protection, we had to move him around regularly. I met with Frank hundreds of times during the following months in various locations across the country, including while he was in prison serving his sentence. Frank was treated courteously and our discussions were always civil in nature."

Cullotta Outed

"We tried to keep Cullotta's defection a secret," former Strike Force lawyer Stan Hunterton said. "We were doing okay until Frank provided information that one of the other Hole in the Wall Gang burglars, Ernie Davino, had fallen out of favor with Spilotro and was going to be killed by one of his colleagues. The alleged hit man was in jail, but was trying to get out on bail pending an appeal of his conviction. We contested the motion, of course. During the bail hearing, Charlie Parsons testified and had to divulge that the source of our information was Frank Cullotta. A gasp went up from the spectators in the courtroom. The word was out, generating a buzz in the media."

The hit man who Frank Cullotta said planned to kill Ernie Davino was fellow HITWG burglar Lawrence Neumann.

Neumann was a very dangerous man. He'd been convicted of a triple murder in Chicago in 1956. In that incident he used a shotgun to kill a bartender, one Max Epstein. He then tried to kill the bartender's brother Mickey, missed and blew away a female employee instead. When leaving the bar, Neumann bumped into a newspaper vendor named John Keller and killed him too. The local papers reported that the slayings were the result of a dispute in which Neumann thought he had been short-changed in the amount of $2. After the dispute he left the bar, returned with the shotgun, and opened fire. He was sentenced to 125 years in prison. For all practical purposes that should have been the end of Mr. Neumann's criminal career. Incredibly, though, the killer was paroled in 1968, after serving only about 11 years of his prison term.

Frank Cullotta was also doing time in the same facility as Neumann and the two became acquainted. According to Cullotta, Neumann was a killer, plain and simple. He kept in top physical condition by exercising daily and "would dismantle you finger by finger." In later years, Neumann intimidated even the ferocious Tony Spilotro himself. Cullotta recalls Spilotro saying of Neumann: "Jesus, don't ever unleash that bastard on me."

Stan Hunterton knew that as long as Neumann remained free, he posed a threat to the public in general and to potential witnesses in particular. He also knew that Frank Cullotta was providing information that would eventually put Neumann away for a long, long time. What Hunterton needed to do was get a conviction against Neumann that would keep him locked up until he could be prosecuted on the new charges. To accomplish that goal, he went after Neumann on the still-unresolved 1981 charge of an ex-felon in possession of a concealed weapon. The gangster was convicted and sentenced to two years, the maximum sentence allowed at that time. During the appeal process from this conviction, Neumann was trying to attain bail so he could kill Davino. Bail was denied, and Neumann was subsequently convicted of murder in 1983 and put away for good.

As more people became aware of the Cullotta situation, the concerns for his safety increased. "Frank was one of the best protected witnesses I ever dealt with," Hunterton added. "He had a lot of information we were interested in. He was a valuable asset and was treated as such."

Differing Opinions

Cullotta also had a lot of baggage. He was a career criminal and an admitted killer who had turned against his friends and associates to get a better deal for himself. How credible a witness would he be?

When Oscar Goodman first heard about Cullotta cooperating with the authorities, he dismissed the matter as a non-event. He told a reporter that he wasn't concerned about Cullotta saying anything detrimental about Tony Spilotro, because there wasn't anything detrimental to say. He added that Tony wished his old pal the best. Goodman further supported his client in a 1983 *Los Angeles Times* article. He said Spilotro was a gentleman, and, "He's never lied to me ... [but] I don't ask him things I may not want to know the answer to. I'm a need-to-know lawyer."

The attorney had a somewhat different take on Cullotta when he later summed up the informant's effectiveness as a government witness. Goodman told author John L. Smith: "Although you'll never get them to admit it, the government never got squat in the way of convictions for turning Frank Cullotta. He admitted murdering four people and his testimony was useless, because he refused to tell the truth. If he told the truth, he would have had to admit that Tony called him a little girl. Nobody in Tony's world trusted Cullotta, because all their lives he'd always been a little girl. It's why even people like Herbie Blitzstein and so many other people in Tony's life all warned him about Cullotta."

The lawmen who worked with Cullotta totally disagree with Goodman's analysis. In their opinion, Cullotta was honest in his dealings with them and his information and testimony resulted in numerous convictions. "We didn't just take his word for things. Everything he told us was corroborated independently. If it couldn't be verified, we didn't use it," Dennis Arnoldy explained. "We learned early on that Frank didn't answer every question by telling us what he thought we wanted to hear. If he didn't know about a specific incident, he'd say he didn't know. When he did tell us something, we'd double- or triple-check it. In that regard, Frank Cullotta was honest with us."

One of the methods used to check Cullotta's veracity was by matching police reports with his claims of criminal activity. For example, Cullotta supplied the date and location of a burglary and the items taken. Records were then searched for an incident report confirming Cullotta's statement and the witness was actually driven to the location to positively identify the site. In a couple of cases involving residential entries, they found that the burglars had actually been under surveillance at the time of the crime. But the crooks had been so efficient that officers thought they were in the home on a social call.

All the local newspapers covered the Cullotta story. Reporters said that anonymous sources "close to the investigation" told them Cullotta was spilling the beans on everything from burglaries and robberies to murder. And his information wasn't limited to Las Vegas. It went back to Chicago and elsewhere. Local mobsters and others from across the country had to be squirming, the journalists speculated.

However, Cullotta's revelations weren't solely about what he and other mobsters had done. He was also talking about those who had facilitated the burglaries and robberies by identifying lucrative targets and providing information about the victim's movements. The valet parkers, desk clerks, dealers, maids, and, in some cases, the casino executives who had been complicit must have also been sweating.

Sheriff McCarthy compared Cullotta's deciding to become a government witness with similar decisions by Jimmy Fratiano and Joseph Valichi. He said Cullotta was having a rippling effect on those in the Mafia all across the country. "It's opened up a new facet to organized crime being involved and tied to a lot of crimes—something many law-enforcement professionals, including myself, didn't understand."

Cullotta's Overall Effectiveness

Contrary to Mr. Goodman's assessment, Frank Cullotta was a very productive cooperating witness, according to Dennis Arnoldy. The former agent believes you have to look beyond Bertha's to properly evaluate Cullotta's overall benefit to the government.

To support his argument, Arnoldy cites statistics of Cullotta's productivity between 1982 and 1988. During that time, Cullotta's testimony in front of various federal and state grand juries and trials was instrumental in obtaining a number of indictments and convictions: 19 federal racketeering-related indictments, four Illinois murder indictments, and five Nevada burglary and armed-robbery indictments. These charges resulted in 15 federal convictions, one Illinois murder conviction, and five Nevada burglary and armed-robbery convictions.

In addition, Cullotta testified before the President's Commission on Organized Crime, the Florida Governor's Commission on Organized Crime, and at a sentencing hearing for Chicago mobster Joseph Lombardo.

The turning of Frank Cullotta impacted on many people in one way or another. To the law-enforcement personnel who brought it about, it made the endless hours of surveillance, interviewing, confrontations, and risk-taking all worthwhile. To many of their opponents, it meant the beginning of the end. To Tony Spilotro, his former friend's move increased the already tremendous pressure he was under. But Tony was a tough guy and he still had some fight left in him.

More Scandals and Allegations

Starting in June, Metro and Kent Clifford were hit with back-to-back charges. In the first incident a former Metro detective was arrested by Intelligence Bureau officers and charged with operating a burglary ring that preyed on drug dealers. The suspect, Larry Gandy, and his crew allegedly identified drug dealers, then broke into their residences to steal money, jewelry, and drugs. Gandy denied that there were any other current or former officers involved.

The news media pounced on the story. During an interview with Gandy, the arrestee claimed that while he worked for Clifford, his boss had once ordered him to rough up a criminal suspect. Gandy claimed he complied by breaking the suspect's nose. Metro denied the allegation.

"Gandy's story was incredible, because he never worked for me; I never had any supervisory authority over him. Of course, the facts couldn't be allowed to stand in the way of a good story," Clifford said in 2004.

He went on to give his version of events. "I met Larry Gandy when we both worked for the former Las Vegas Police Department. I was a fairly new cop at the time and Gandy was one of the stars of the department. He had a reputation as being a good narcotics officer, but a little crazy. I took Gandy's place in the narcotics unit when he left to take a job with the State of Nevada Narcotics Division. We worked a couple of joint investigations together and shared intelligence information on dope dealers. I think we considered ourselves to be friends. But he eventually left law enforcement and became a bail bondsman, and then a burglar and dope dealer. We arrested him in 1982 for burglarizing the house of a citizen who had an ounce of cocaine for personal use. I believe that Gandy found out about the dope from the dealer who had sold it and he wanted to steal it and resell it.

"His method of operation was to have a flunky kick in the front door of the target's residence and enter to make sure nobody was home. If it was clear, Gandy would come in and do the burglary. We had intelligence that he had done the same thing in California. When the front man went inside, he was confronted by an armed homeowner and blown away. A vehicle matching Gandy's was spotted leaving the scene, but there was no positive ID.

"The guy he was using as a front man in Vegas, a guy he abused regularly, came to me and told me what was going on. We arrested Gandy during the commission of the burglary. I told him I felt betrayed and said I felt like kicking his ass. I didn't say I was going to do it, just that I felt like it. On the way to the jail, he offered to become an informant and turn us on to some big dope dealers if we turned him loose. I refused to deal with him because of the way I felt about him and booked him. Two days later that story appeared in the newspaper. I didn't respond to it, because it was the ranting of a burglar and dope dealer. Gandy was unable to identify the victim of the alleged assault and nothing came of it. I chalked it up to sour grapes and went about my work."

Another shoe dropped when a Metro detective charged that Clifford had permitted a confidential informant to sell cocaine on the street three years earlier. According to the allegation, the informant had purchased three ounces of cocaine from a casino executive and turned the information and drugs over to Clifford. He wanted to be reimbursed for the purchase. The Intelligence Bureau chief didn't want to pay $2,500 for what he thought was a weak case. On the other hand, he didn't want to lose a valuable informant. As a compromise, Clifford allegedly told the informant to sell the drugs and get his money back.

This charge was also denied by Metro and attributed to McCarthy's political adversaries getting an early start on the election campaign. When reporters questioned John Moran about the timing of the accusation, he denied having any role in the release of the information.

In late July, the District Attorney's office announced that there was insufficient information to charge Clifford with any wrongdoing in the cocaine case. Metro officers opposed to McCarthy claimed the decision not to prosecute was a whitewash. McCarthy maintained that the allegations were unfounded and politically motivated.

This was another case in which the accused says the newspaper accounts didn't match the facts. "The amount of cocaine involved was actually one ounce, not three," Kent Clifford said. "By Nevada law, an officer could trade or sell an ounce of narcotics as long as it was done in a controlled situation. We traded the ounce of cocaine for an ounce of heroin to get into a drug dealer. An arrest was subsequently made in the case. Someone in the Intelligence Bureau knew bits and pieces of the deal and told one of John Moran's cronies. As the story circulated, everything was blown out of proportion. The newspapers ran with it and never contacted me to find out what was really going on. My relationship with the DA's office wasn't very good then. They cleared me, because I hadn't done anything wrong. There was no whitewash."

The Campaign Officially Begins

In September, Sheriff McCarthy and John Moran won their respective primaries. The charges began to fly almost immediately. Frank Cullotta got into the fray by stating that Tony Spilotro had donated $40,000 to the Moran campaign and supplied booze for his campaign parties. Moran emphatically denied Cullotta's claims, calling them "out-and-out lies." He blamed the allegations on dirty tricks by the McCarthy people. Two days later Moran announced that he had taken a polygraph test that proved Cullotta's story was baseless. He also suggested that Sheriff McCarthy submit to a polygraph examination regarding the old allegations that Spilotro had contributed to McCarthy's campaign of four years earlier.

For his part, McCarthy admitted having heard about the accusations, but denied having anything to do with their becoming public.

In early October, Moran came under additional fire for dropping out of a scheduled debate with McCarthy on KLAS-TV. He claimed that one of the panelists was a staunch McCarthy supporter, so he wouldn't get a fair shake.

The allegation game became a two-way street a week later when McCarthy was accused of receiving a $2,000 donation from Joe Conforte, a fugitive Nevada brothel owner, during his 1978 campaign against Ralph Lamb. McCarthy admitted receiving the money, but said it was made by a third party and the identity of the actual donor was never known to him. The person who had kept the campaign's books at the time said the donation had been in the form of a cashier's check. The man who had actually made the contribution on behalf of Conforte disputed that, saying it'd been a cash transaction. No record of that donation was found on file with the Secretary of State.

On October 20, McCarthy attacked Moran's character in a newspaper article. He accused his opponent of conducting a campaign based on slanted commercials and fraudulent statements to the press. "I wonder what else he's lying about to deceive the people of Clark County," McCarthy said.

Moran wasted little time in responding. He challenged both McCarthy and Clifford to take a polygraph exam to prove they hadn't been responsible for leaking the allegation that Spilotro had made a contribution to his campaign. Both men declined his invitation, stating that the charges were a matter between Moran and Cullotta. As October neared an end, the news for Sheriff McCarthy wasn't good. Polls showed that the incumbent was pulling only 29% of the vote.

Lefty's Big Bang

Rosenthal's stock with the Chicago Outfit and Tony Spilotro had been dwindling for some time. His highly publicized fight with the gaming authorities and his controversial television show hadn't gone over very well in Chicago or with some of the other crime families. And the fiasco over Tony's affair with Geri caused the bosses to be concerned about the judgment of both men. Spilotro was unhappy with his former buddy, because Lefty hadn't backed his play to expand his power in Vegas and California. The situation with Geri had placed a further wedge between them.

Nick Civella, boss of the Kansas City mob that controlled the Tropicana, had been suspicious of Lefty for some time. He believed the gambler was way too friendly with the FBI and might be acting as an informant. At one point Civella called Oscar Goodman and asked if he thought Lefty was crazy. The lawyer said he didn't think Rosenthal was crazy, that he was okay. An FBI agent later testified at the mob chief's racketeering trial that to Civella, "crazy" was code for "trustworthy."

Goodman said he wasn't aware of the dual meaning at the time. When he learned about it, he realized that had he given the wrong answer, Lefty might have been killed. Still, was Rosenthal providing the authorities with information?

Attorney Goodman explained it this way: "There are snitches and then there are snitches. There is such a thing as a dry snitch, a person who talks to the FBI or police, but doesn't necessarily say anything. I think Frank Rosenthal enjoyed playing with people in power. I think a lot of people played the game with him. But did he sit down and say, 'Make a deal for me not to be prosecuted'? I don't think so. I think he'd been through too much in his life to become a rat."

The mob bosses may not have been sufficiently convinced that Lefty needed to be eliminated. Tony Spilotro was another matter. In mid-September, Metro picked up word that the Ant had ordered Lefty killed. Similar to the policy of their FBI colleagues, the cops were required to inform the potential victim that he was in danger. Gene Smith and his partner were tasked with telling Rosenthal.

"We found Lefty in a restaurant with some of his buddies," Smith said. "I told him we'd like to talk with him in private. He said no. The other men were his friends and anything we had to say could be said in front of them. Under those circumstances, I said, 'Okay, you're going to be killed.' We turned around and walked out, with a suddenly interested Lefty right on our heels. Outside the restaurant we told him the whole story. He didn't believe it, though. We'd done what we had to do. Our obligation to Lefty was over."

A couple of weeks later on the evening of October 4, Rosenthal left Tony Roma's restaurant on East Sahara. He got into his Cadillac and turned the key in the ignition. In the past, this action had always resulted in the Caddy's engine coming to life and settling into a smooth purr. Things were a bit different this time. A charge of C-4 explosive had been placed under the trunk next to the gas tank and wired to the ignition. When Lefty turned the key the bomb ignited. Had he been in any other car, the gambler would no doubt have been killed instantly. But the Caddy was built with a steel plate under the driver's seat as standard equipment. The steel barrier diverted the blast toward the passenger side of the vehicle and gave Lefty a chance to jump out of the car before the interior became fully engulfed. The gas tank exploded seconds later, sending the car's roof 60 feet into the air. The lucky Lefty escaped the inferno with only some singed clothes and minor injuries. He was alive, but someone had sent a strong message.

The day after the bombing, Rosenthal called Metro and demanded police protection. Kent Clifford and Gene Smith went to Lefty's house to discuss the situation. "I asked him what he'd do for us in return for protecting him," Kent Clifford said. "His answer was, 'Nothing.' I told him I wasn't going to put my men at risk under those circumstances. I tried to scare him into talking to us or the FBI by telling him he was a walking dead man. He decided to take his chances rather than cooperate, though."

Who was responsible for the attempt on Lefty's life? The theories varied among the lawmen. Those who believed Tony Spilotro was behind the incident admitted that the Ant wasn't known for using explosives. But they argued that he had motive and could have brought in an outside expert to handle the bombing. Others thought Chicago, with pressure from Kansas City, had ordered the hit, because they felt Lefty was either already in bed with the authorities or soon would be. Those who supported this idea pointed out that car bombings were common in assassinations by mob families throughout the Midwest.

Some outside of law enforcement attributed Lefty's near-death experience to Geri Rosenthal's friends in California. Their rationale was that Geri was rapidly going through the money she'd left Las Vegas with. Her friends—comprised primarily of drug users, dealers, and biker gang members—believed she stood to gain a windfall from Lefty's estate should he suffer a premature demise. In that case, the free-spending Geri would be able to support their bad habits for the foreseeable future. Therefore, it made sense that these unsavory characters would attempt to knock Lefty off.

Not long after the bombing, the gambler departed Las Vegas for California, and eventually Florida. Like so many of the killings and attempted killings in the realm of the mobsters, no one was ever charged in the attack.

The End for Geri

Just over a month after her ex-husband narrowly escaped death, Geri Rosenthal's life ended in California. On November 6, she stumbled into a seedy Sunset Boulevard motel and started screaming, then fell unconscious to the floor. She was transported to a hospital, but died three days later without coming out of her coma. The coroner ruled her death was the result of an accidental drug overdose. The cash and jewelry she had left Las Vegas with were never found, apparently having been spent, stolen, or both.

Kent Clifford and other involved law enforcers don't necessarily believe in coincidence, or that the coroner's findings in Geri Rosenthal's case were completely accurate. "A skilled hit man can very easily administer a lethal dose of drugs and make it appear as though the deceased accidentally did it himself," Clifford said. "Geri had been married to Lefty and sleeping with Tony. She knew a lot and she was a druggie. That combination made her a potential threat to a lot of people. It's my opinion that she was murdered, but in such a way that it will remain impossible to prove." Many of Clifford's former colleagues agree with his assessment.

McCarthy Defeated

After an exceptionally bitter campaign, John Moran defeated John McCarthy at the ballot box on November 2 to become the sheriff-elect of Clark County. One of Moran's main campaign promises was that he would bring the prostitution problem under control within 90 days of taking office. He fulfilled that promise.

Sheriff Moran also continued the department's aggressive fight against organized crime, minus some of the familiar faces. Kent Clifford left Metro at the end of McCarthy's term. Gene Smith stayed on, but he and some of the other detectives were transferred out of the Intelligence Bureau and replaced with officers of Moran's choosing.

On December 23, Sheriff McCarthy received a letter from FBI Director William Webster, thanking him for his efforts against organized crime. The Frank Cullotta case and the outstanding cooperation between Metro and the FBI under McCarthy's guidance were specifically mentioned.

Twenty-two years after leaving office, John McCarthy reflected on his term. "I had a lot of disappointment in the outcome of the 1982 election, but I have no regrets. I doubt I would change much if I had it to do over again. The situation required a hard-ass approach to keep others from running all over you. And the harder they got, the more it steeled me.

"Organized crime is so insidious and pervasive that the general public doesn't understand its influence on their everyday lives. Some people in Las Vegas feared that the common criminals would prevail if organized crime wasn't there to keep them in line. They didn't grasp that the mobsters were nothing but common criminals themselves.

"I almost ended up going to jail myself over the Consent Decree. Some of my team wanted me to make a political statement by not complying with the court order and being jailed for contempt. However, in my view there wasn't any option other than to comply, using the full powers of my office. We got the job done and that's all that matters.

"The Intelligence Bureau was a large player in my administration. The outcome of the election resulted in the reorganization of that unit and, in my opinion, took the focus away from the fight against organized crime. I believe that what we worked so hard to accomplish, often at great risk, was diminished to some degree. That was indeed a major regret for me."

Kent Clifford shared his thoughts about his days as the chief of the Intelligence Bureau with the *Review-Journal* in early 1983. "The public often thought organized-crime figures were something special. They weren't. Most of them were street punks. They were common thieves, thugs, murderers, and they scratched and clawed their way to the top. It didn't really take a lot of brains."

Comparing the war on the gangsters to the one in Vietnam, Clifford said, "We [Metro and the FBI] had to play by the rules and within limited budgets. Anybody who can out-finance you and has no rules will give you fits. In Vietnam, we played by the rules and nobody else did. So we didn't win that war."

Clifford cited the turning of Frank Cullotta as one of the high points of Metro's war on organized crime. "Frank Cullotta was a major accomplishment, not only for this department, but for the nation. There are very few local departments who can make that kind of a claim. I think we did very well as an intelligence unit and I have a letter from the director of the FBI commending me for my four years."

Former Commander Clifford also believes that the murder of Allen Dorfman had a Las Vegas connection. "I think why Dorfman was killed is because he had knowledge of everything that was going on in Las Vegas. He knew Spilotro and was a close associate of [Chicago mobster] Joey Lombardo. If Dorfman had lived and become a government informant, he would have shaken Nevada to its roots."

Clifford has a strong opinion that John McCarthy did a good job and deserved another term. "There is no doubt, and nobody can refute this, if there hadn't been a John McCarthy, there wouldn't have been a new jail built in Clark County. If the voters had given him another four years, crime would have decreased significantly."

In summing up, Clifford said, "To erase organized crime will take a national effort, a national opinion that organized crime cannot be tolerated."

Kent Clifford stands by those comments today.

11

Indictment in Chicago

On January 27, 1983, Richard Daley, state's attorney for Cook County, Illinois, and Chicago mayoral candidate, held a press conference. He announced publicly that Tony Spilotro had been indicted for the 1962 torture killings of James Miraglia and William McCarthy, the M&M murders. The indictment was based in large part on the grand-jury testimony of Frank Cullotta. According to Daley, Cullotta had testified that he helped Tony set up the slayings, but hadn't actually been present when the murders were committed. Following the press conference, Spilotro was arrested in Las Vegas and jailed without bail to await extradition to Illinois.

Oscar Goodman learned of Tony's troubles when he returned to Vegas after winning a major, but unrelated, case in Florida. He rushed from the airport to his office, then over to the jail to see his client. A few hours later the accused murderer was released on bail. Goodman's ability to spring a client facing extradition on such serious charges raised some eyebrows in law enforcement and legal circles. Before the case was settled, Spilotro's bail wouldn't be the only thing to cause bewilderment.

The Ant and Goodman spent a substantial amount of time preparing for the trial. In Chicago they conferred regularly with Herb Barsky, an attorney who had long represented Spilotro in the Windy City. Barsky had the reputation of knowing how to work the system and being able to get things done.

When Judge Thomas J. Maloney was assigned to hear the case, both Barsky and Spilotro were pleased. In fact, they were so impressed with Judge Maloney that they suggested to Goodman they should forego a jury trial and let Maloney decide Tony's guilt or innocence. It was an idea that didn't initially sit well with the Las Vegas attorney.

Goodman explained his feelings about trying a murder case without a jury to author John L. Smith: "Tony liked the idea, but in my career I'd tried it only once, and that was in Las Vegas at the insistence of a client who was up on income–tax charges and had drawn Harry Claiborne as a judge in federal court. I knew Harry. The client knew Harry. He insisted they were close friends and that the judge would never rule against him because of that friendship. I refused at first, but he insisted. And I'm convinced that Claiborne was harder on him than he would have been had my client taken a damn jury trial. Claiborne convicted him and threw the book at him."

In spite of his misgivings, Goodman went along with the wishes of Spilotro and Barsky. However, his preparation was virtually the same as it would have been if Tony were being judged by a jury of his peers. He believed the government's chief witness, Frank Cullotta, whom the lawyer called the "King Rat," was a liar and would lie on the stand. He planned to use Cullotta's record, including his admission to the Lisner murder, to discredit and neutralize his testimony.

Trying Times

Back in Las Vegas, Vincent Spilotro closely followed his father's case, which was broadcast on Chicago TV station WGN. While the teenager watched the television, he engaged in another pastime he had come to enjoy: drinking alcohol.

As the son of the reputed Las Vegas crime kingpin, Vincent had experienced a rather unique childhood. He was usually well-heeled financially and able to do things that most kids his age weren't. While his status could be viewed as beneficial in many cases, it also had some pitfalls. One of them was the ease with which he could get involved with vices such as booze. Vincent developed a taste for Jack Daniels and it became his drink of choice. He wasn't exactly a social drinker, either. By the time of the M&M trial, the young Spilotro could polish off a fifth of JD in just a few hours. As the case unfolded, Vincent was under a great deal of stress. He relieved some of that anxiety by the use of his bottled ally.

"I'm watching my dad's trial on TV and hearing that he could get the death penalty if convicted. I couldn't go to school. I was paralyzed. I sat at home watching and drinking a bottle of Jack Daniels. But he called me every day," Vincent recalled. He later heard those conversations when they were replayed on law-enforcement wiretap tapes.

But after all the evidence was in and the judge was deliberating, Tony didn't call. "So I'm drunk. I'm holding a bottle of Jack Daniels and I call him. I screamed at him because he didn't call from the courthouse."

For Vincent, this was a period of torment. But his father, the man whose life was on the line, remained calm, cool, and upbeat. He exhibited none of the anxiety attacks and heart trouble that later kept him in bed for days at a time. On the contrary, in Chicago Tony arose early, ate well, and showed his lawyer around the Windy City during the evening. Did the Ant know something his son didn't?

Acquittal

Tony Spilotro was acquitted of the charges against him. After careful deliberation, Judge Maloney ruled that the prosecution hadn't proved its case beyond a reasonable doubt. According to Goodman, as quoted in John L. Smith's *Of Rats and Men*, the decision was somewhat of a surprise to him.

"In Illinois courts, after the prosecution rests its case, it's common for the defense to file a motion to dismiss due to a lack of evidence. In Tony's case, it was obvious the prosecution suffered from a lack of evidence. I made what I thought was an excellent argument and the judge ruled against me. I was devastated. In my mind, I'd clearly shown the flaws in the case. It left me taken aback a bit. I wasn't going to put Tony on the stand. I was really worried.

"I said to Tony, 'We're history.' Tony said, 'Don't worry about it.'

"In retrospect, it should have made me wonder more than it did at the time. I was too worried about putting on a defense. The defense was brief. Obviously, my client hadn't been at the scene of the crime and Frank Cullotta was a proven liar. I had shown that much when I cross-examined him. I had a sleepless night, which is usual for me, prior to making the closing argument in the case. The prosecution got to go last. Finally, the judge came back and ruled the prosecution hadn't proved guilt beyond a reasonable doubt."

It looked as though Oscar Goodman had worked his courtroom magic once again. But there were questions. Had Goodman's skills really been necessary or had the outcome of the trial been pre-determined?

Judge Maloney

In 1993, ten years after the M&M trial, Thomas Maloney, the presiding judge, had the dubious distinction of being the only Illinois judge ever convicted of fixing a murder case.

Although Maloney wasn't charged in conjunction with the Spilotro trial, a closer look at his history and the Chicago court system of the time may help explain why Spilotro and Barsky insisted on foregoing a jury trial and why Tony wasn't overly concerned when Goodman's motion to dismiss was denied.

Thomas Maloney was a practicing defense attorney in Chicago in 1977 when he was appointed by the Illinois Supreme Court to fill a vacancy in the Circuit Court. One year later, he ran for that office and was elected by the voters. Maloney retained the position until his retirement in 1990.

In the early 1980s, the feds launched Operation Greylord, designed to investigate suspicions of corruption in the Chicago courts. One of the key players in a subsequent probe, Operation Gambat, which began in 1986, was Robert Cooley, a Chicago criminal defense lawyer in the 1970s and '80s. Cooley represented, and fixed cases for, organized-crime figures. He was very successful in purchasing influence in the courts and didn't lose a case for approximately four years.

"I had no problem paying people money to make sure I got a decision in a case. In fact, I wanted to win all my cases and I did," Cooley explained. But all that changed in the late 1980s when a client asked the attorney to arrange to have a witness murdered. That's when Robert Cooley became an FBI informant.

As a result of Operations Greylord and Gambat, 92 individuals, including defense attorneys, bailiffs, clerks, and 13 judges, were indicted. One of those 13 was Thomas Maloney. Maloney was convicted in 1993 on charges of racketeering conspiracy, racketeering, extortion under color of official right, and obstruction of justice. These violations of the law all arose from three cases in which Judge Maloney took bribes in cases before him. In 1994 he was sentenced to 15 years in prison and fined $200,000.

The first of the three cases took place in 1981. In that instance, three hit men were accused of attempted murder.

During the course of the trial, the victim died and the charges were elevated to murder. Defense attorney Robert Cooley was retained by political friends of the defendants and assured that Judge Maloney could be bought, but that the price would be high. The politicians contributed $100,000 to grease the various hands involved in the fix, including Maloney's. At trial, the judge admitted as evidence a dying declaration from the victim identifying the defendants as his killers. But he then ruled that the declaration was unreliable, resulting in acquittals for all three defendants. After turning informant, Cooley covertly taped a conversation with one of the politicians who acknowledged the case had been fixed.

The next charged bribe occurred in 1982 and was also a murder case. This time a single defendant and a different defense attorney were involved. Maloney wasn't able to let the defendant off completely, because the case was receiving a lot of media attention and was considered too hot for an out-and-out acquittal. But that didn't mean the judge couldn't be of service. As a compromise, Maloney offered to acquit on felony murder, convict on voluntary manslaughter, and impose a nine-year sentence. That outcome was preferable to the sentence of at least 20 years that would have resulted from a murder conviction and the deal was made. After a trial before Judge Maloney, the defendant was convicted of the lesser charge and received the promised nine-year sentence.

The final charged bribe was in a 1985 case and consisted of two defendants accused of murdering two men. This time the fix was arranged, but it didn't come to fruition. A middleman negotiated a fee of $10,000 for the defendants to receive acquittals after a bench trial. Things fell apart when the prosecution put on such a strong case—including three credible eyewitnesses to the murders—that Judge Maloney saw no way he could let the defendants off. Through the middleman, he sent word that he was going to return the bribe money. Maloney was talked into hanging on to the cash until the defense put on its case. If they could discredit the government's evidence, perhaps Maloney could still deliver. The defense flopped. Maloney found both men guilty and sentenced them to death.

Do these incidents mean conclusively that the Spilotro trial was fixed? No, they don't. They simply raise a possibility that can logically be considered. But at least two people believe that Tony was in no danger when he faced Judge Maloney.

On November 11, 2003, Las Vegas TV station KVBC aired a segment on its nightly news show called "Another Side of Oscar Goodman." The focus of the piece was the M&M murder trial, whether Tony Spilotro had beaten the rap due to a crooked judge and, if so, had Goodman been aware of it. One of the guests interviewed by reporter Glen Meek was former mob lawyer-turned-informant Robert Cooley. The following dialogue took place between Meek and Cooley:

Meek to Cooley: Was the murder case involving Mr. Spilotro fixed?

Cooley: Absolutely it was fixed. Any of the murderers, any other of the organized-crime people, if they got arrested and indicted, their cases would be assigned to Tom Maloney and he would throw the cases out. He was the one that was … they got Tony Spilotro's case assigned to him. I cannot see an attorney representing someone like Tony Spilotro taking a bench trial unless he knew the result.

Meek [narrative]: In a new biography by John L. Smith, Goodman says he agreed to a bench trial because his Chicago co-counsel suggested it and Spilotro insisted. The Chicago lawyer—who is now deceased—was an attorney in another case in front of Maloney that was also allegedly fixed. Maloney ultimately found Spilotro not guilty.

Cooley: Tony, well, Tony was laughing about it. I mean, I saw Tony on many occasions before and after. I mean, Tony made it clear the case was fixed and he had no problems with the case.

Meek [narrative]: Though Maloney was never charged

with taking a bribe in the Spilotro murder trial, it did surface during Maloney's sentencing for fixing other cases. But the evidence was not deemed sufficient to increase Maloney's prison term.

What does Mr. Goodman have to say about this? Mayor Goodman declined an on-camera interview, saying, quote, "I'm not going to give any credence to some jerk shooting his mouth off."

By phone, Goodman said of the Spilotro trial: All I can tell you is if it was fixed, I never knew it. I tried my heart out in that case.

Robert Cooley remains convinced Spilotro's murder trial was rigged.

Meek to Cooley: Is it likely in your opinion that his attorney, Oscar Goodman—who is now mayor of Las Vegas—didn't know it was fixed?

Cooley: Well, it's possible I'll be seven-foot tall when I wake up in the morning. But the odds are pretty good against it [end interview].

Joe Yablonsky, the former Las Vegas FBI chief, had earlier expressed his reservations about the legitimacy of the M&M trial. In his letter to the editor of the *Las Vegas Review-Journal* in April 1999, Yablonsky, talking about Oscar Goodman, said:

"Why did he and his co-counsel in Chicago waive a jury in the M&M boys' homicide case (the victim's head was placed in a vise, popping his eyeballs) perpetrated by his beloved client, "gentle" Tony "the Ant" Spilotro? Waiving a jury trial in a homicide case is virtually unheard of. It places the fate of the defendant in the judgment of one person, the judge, as opposed to 12 jurors. The judge in that case was subsequently convicted of corruption in an FBI sting operation known as Greylord."

More Troubles for Tony

Whatever the true circumstances of the M&M trial, Tony Spilotro was in the clear once more and free to refocus his attention on Las Vegas. And he had more problems awaiting him there. During the Chicago trial, Tony was charged in the 1979 murder of Jerry Lisner. This was another case brought as the result of testimony from Frank Cullotta. Although Cullotta had admitted pulling the trigger, he said that he was acting under Spilotro's orders. Even with everything Tony had going against him at the time and the seriousness of the charges, Goodman was able to arrange for his client to stay free on his own recognizance on the new charges. On top of that, he made the agreement via a long-distance phone call from Chicago to Las Vegas, surprising most of those following Spilotro's exploits.

Oscar Goodman himself had a lot on his plate other than Spilotro. In one of his major pending cases, the feds were hot on the trail of Allen Glick and his Argent-controlled casinos. The noose was tightening and a strategy to fight the government had to be developed.

Both warriors headed back to Nevada to prepare for the battles ahead.

12

The Skim

Much has been written and there have been several documentaries about various organized-crime families taking cash—"skimming"—from Las Vegas casinos. The skim money was removed from the casino prior to it officially being entered into the books as revenue. Taxes weren't paid on this unreported income, a fact on which the Internal Revenue Service frowned. The casinos involved in these illegal operations became the equivalent of piggy banks for the Midwest crime bosses.

I'd read and seen accounts of how the skims worked, but I never fully appreciated the operation until I researched the subject for this book. Perhaps my lack of interest and understanding was due to looking at it as merely financial crimes, without realizing the amount of violence and intimidation involved to launch and maintain the scams. Or maybe it was because I'd failed to delve into the immense investigative effort it took to bring the perpetrators before the bar of justice.

Whatever the reason, as I learned that several of the murders attributed to Tony Spilotro involved protecting organized-crime's casino interests, my attitude changed. This wasn't just about financial wrongdoing. In fact, if it weren't for the mob's hidden ownership of and control over the casinos and the need to protect the status quo, there may never have been a Tony Spilotro and his gang in Las Vegas.

So, although Tony wasn't one of the inside men in the casinos, the skim operations were part and parcel of the Spilotro era.

Two major investigations, called Strawman 1 and 2, involved the casinos owned by Argent Corporation, as well as the Tropicana. Many of the same players were involved with both, but the courts ruled that these were separate conspiracies. There were separate indictments, trials, and convictions. Some of the participants entered into plea deals and testified against their colleagues. Others gave testimony as unindicted co-conspirators. Several top mobsters from the Midwest went to prison.

A continuation of the Strawman investigations was called Strawman-Trans Sterling. This operation zeroed in on the Trans Sterling Corporation, another mob-controlled company that purchased Argent's casino holdings and resulted in more gangsters going to prison.

From a law-enforcement standpoint, these investigations and subsequent convictions marked the end of organized crime's influence over the Las Vegas casinos.

The Families

Four Midwest organized-crime families were involved in the hidden ownership and skimming of the Argent-controlled casinos and the Tropicana: Chicago, Kansas City, Milwaukee, and Cleveland. They each had ownership and control and/or participated in the illegal removal of cash from the involved gaming establishments. Although all four shared in the money taken from the Tropicana, the courts ruled that it was a Kansas City operation and that the other three families weren't involved in the covert ownership of that casino.

Allen Glick's Argent Corporation was a different story than the Tropicana. Glick had a clean criminal record and could withstand the background check conducted by Nevada gaming regulators. So being the owner of record of multiple casinos wouldn't be a problem. But he needed a large amount of money in order to purchase the Stardust, Fremont, Hacienda, and Marina. And at a time when not many reputable financial institutions were willing to invest in Vegas, the best source of that funding was the Teamster Central States Pension Fund (CSPF). Three of the four families—Milwaukee, Kansas City, and Cleveland—held influence over one or more of the CSPF trustees or union officials. Since any one trustee could veto the loans, cooperation among the families was necessary to assure the trustees and officials were all on board and that Glick got the money he needed. In return for their assistance in obtaining the funding, the families had effective control of Argent, with Glick serving as their front man. Shortly after the skim began, a dispute developed between Kansas City and Milwaukee. Chicago intervened and resolved the matter, then joined the conspiracy, taking a 25% cut of the action.

For the mobsters, it began as a marriage made in heaven. For gaming authorities and law enforcement, it was a nightmare. The lawmen came to realize that like a malignant tumor, the influence of organized crime in the Las Vegas casinos had to be cut out and destroyed. However, once the malignancy had taken root, removing it was easier said than done.

The Main Mob Players

The Chicago Outfit was the dominant family operating in Las Vegas. The two most powerful mobsters in Chicago at that time were Joe Aiuppa and Tony Accardo, the same men who had sent Tony Spilotro to Vegas. In addition, other members involved in the family's Las Vegas business dealings were underboss John Cerone, West Side boss Joseph "Joey the Clown" Lombardo, Angelo LaPietra, and Allen Dorfman.

Kansas City, under the leadership of Nick Civella and his brother Carl, contributed underboss Carl "Tuffy" DeLuna, Anthony Chiavola, Sr., and Joe Agosto to the conspiracies. Although Chiavola resided in Chicago, he was a nephew of the Civella brothers and was more closely associated with their group.

Nick Civella was born Guiseppe Civello in Kansas City in 1927. At the age of 10 he was brought before juvenile authorities for "incorrigibility." By the time he was 20, Nick had dropped out of school and had a lengthy arrest record for crimes such as car theft, gambling, and robbery. In 1957 he attended the infamous "gangland convention" in Apalachin, New York.

Due to his criminal history, Nick Civella was among the first people to be placed in Nevada's "black book," barring him from entering Nevada's casinos. Undeterred by his exclusion, Civella frequently visited Las Vegas wearing wigs and fake beards to fool state gaming officials. During these forays, he usually stayed at the Tropicana or Dunes.

In Milwaukee, boss Frank "Frankie Bal" Balistrieri was the first mobster to be contacted by Allen Glick regarding the Teamster loans for Argent. Balistrieri's mob had control of the loansharking, bookmaking, and vending-machine businesses in their city. Balistrieri himself had been convicted of income-tax evasion in 1967 and served two years in federal prison. During Frank's absence, Peter Balistrieri, his brother and underboss, ran the show.

Milton Rockman represented Cleveland. He served as a bagman for the delivery of the purloined money and as a liaison person for Kansas City's Carl DeLuna.

These talented criminals and their minions put together a plan that took millions of dollars from Las Vegas and put them into their own pockets.

Nick and Roy

In addition to his clout in Kansas City and with other mobsters around the country, Nick Civella had something else working for him: He was able to influence the decisions of the Teamster Central States Pension Fund through his control of Roy Williams, a Teamster official and its eventual president.

Williams, a decorated World War II combat veteran, returned to Kansas City after the war and resumed his job as a truck driver. He also became heavily involved in the Teamsters and rose through the leadership ranks with the backing of another rising star, Jimmy Hoffa.

Hoffa picked Williams to take over a troubled local in Wichita, and later Kansas City's Local 41. It was then that he met Nick Civella and they became close personal friends. In 1952, Williams attended a secret meeting of Midwest mob leaders in Chicago, where Williams agreed to run the Kansas City Teamsters and in turn cooperate with his organized-crime friends. Williams discussed all major union problems with Civella before making a decision. If the two men couldn't agree on a subject, Hoffa ordered Williams to "do what Nick wants."

Hoffa was pleased with the way Williams worked with Civella and followed instructions. He rewarded his underling by appointing him as a trustee of the Central States Pension Fund. It was a powerful position, and Nick Civella certainly approved of his lackey occupying it.

When Frank Balistrieri needed help in assuring Argent got the Teamster money it needed, he knew Nick Civella would be able to deliver.

Argent

Allen R. Glick was born in Pittsburgh, Pennsylvania, in 1942. He served in the military as a helicopter pilot during the war in Vietnam and later turned up in the San Diego area as a land developer. In early 1974, Glick contacted Frank Balistrieri in Milwaukee, seeking assistance in obtaining loans from the Central States Pension Fund to finance Argent's purchase of several Las Vegas casinos. Balistrieri brought Kansas City and Cleveland into the deal, with Chicago joining a short time later, in order to assure that the CSPF trustees whom they controlled would vote the right way. The loan was approved. Between the initial loan of $62 million and subsequent loans, Argent received approximately $146 million in Teamster money.

The financing came with strings attached, of course. After Glick purchased the casinos, he was required to install Frank "Lefty" Rosenthal in a management position at Argent. From that post Rosenthal ran casino operations and facilitated the skim. The Stardust and Fremont were the casinos from which the thefts took place.

Carl DeLuna (Kansas City), an efficient overseer, was assigned to monitor the Vegas action and make sure each family received its fair share of the proceeds. In that role, he was one of the most trusted men in American organized crime. He also maintained regular contact with the other groups through Angelo LaPietra (Chicago) and Milton Rockman (Cleveland). To assure everything was done on the up and up, at least as far as the gangsters were concerned, DeLuna kept records—detailed written records.

The skimmed cash was removed from casino count rooms by couriers with full access to those sensitive areas. These men weren't challenged, or even acknowledged, by other employees as they entered, made their withdrawals, and departed. The currency they took was never logged in and there was no official record of it. For all practical purposes, it was as though the money never existed. The loot was then delivered to LaPietra in Chicago. He kept a portion for the Outfit and passed the balance along to Anthony Chiavola, Sr. and Milton Rockman for delivery to their respective families.

The scheme was relatively simple and went smoothly, at least at the start. But after a while it became apparent that Allen Glick didn't completely realize that he was only a powerless figurehead. He actually believed he could make major decisions regarding casino operations. He tried, and when he and Rosenthal clashed, Glick attempted to fire him. Lefty responded with a threat, prompting the naïve tycoon to complain to Frank Balistrieri. Bad move.

In March 1975, Glick was summoned to Kansas City to meet with Nick Civella. There, the boss explained the facts of life to him. The two men met in a hotel room where Civella announced that Glick owed the Kansas City family $1.2 million for its assistance in getting the CSPF loan approved. If Glick didn't know it before, he quickly became aware that the mobsters considered the pension fund to be their private bank.

Glick later recalled what Civella told him. "Cling to every word I say. ... If it would be my choice you wouldn't leave this room alive. You owe us $1.2 million. I want that paid. In addition, we own part of your corporation and you are not to interfere with it. We will let Mr. Rosenthal continue with the casinos and you are not to interfere."

Welcome to the real world, Mr. Glick.

The following year, Rosenthal started causing problems. His battles with Nevada gaming regulators were not only problematic, they were high-profile. The bosses had a good thing going in Vegas and wanted to stay below the radar screen. The unwanted publicity made some of the higher-ups nervous.

But as the months passed, Lefty's difficulties and the related media coverage only intensified. The bosses held conversations to discuss whether Rosenthal should be replaced and, if so, should the removal be on a permanent basis. Although some favored that resolution, Lefty was allowed to stay on and continue his struggle with the licensing officials.

By March 1978, Allen Glick was getting on everyone's

nerves. He was particularly unpopular with Nick Civella. The Kansas City chief decided that Glick needed to go, but was willing to let him get out while still breathing. A buyout proposal in the amount of $10 million was delivered to Glick through Frank Rosenthal. Glick turned down the offer, another ill-advised decision.

On April 25, Carl DeLuna flew to Las Vegas to give Glick a message from Nick Civella. The Civella family frequently used its attorney's office in Kansas City—without the lawyer himself present—to hold sensitive meetings. They knew there was little chance that the locale would be bugged and they could talk freely. Following that practice, DeLuna, Glick, and Rosenthal got together in Oscar Goodman's office, sans Goodman. Allen Glick later testified about that meeting.

"I entered Mr. Goodman's office and behind Mr. Goodman's desk with his feet up was Mr. DeLuna. Mr. DeLuna, in a gruff voice, using graphic terms, told me to sit down. With that he pulled out a piece of paper from his pocket … and he looked down at the paper for a few seconds. Then he informed me he was sent to deliver one final message from his partners. And then he began reading the paper. He said he and his partners were finally sick of having to deal with me and having me around and that I could no longer be tolerated. He informed me it was their desire to have me sell Argent Corporation immediately and I was to announce that sale as soon as I left Mr. Goodman's office that day. He said he realized that the threats I received perhaps may not have been taken by me as serious as they were given to me. And he said that since perhaps I find my life expendable, he was certain I wouldn't find my children's lives expendable. With that he looked down on his paper and gave me the names and ages of each of my sons."

Less than two months after that meeting, Glick publicly announced his intention to sell Argent. In December 1979, Argent was sold to the Trans Sterling Corporation, another company with mob ties. Although Argent was no longer the licensee, it did remain an entity, thanks to the mortgage it held on the casinos. Kansas City continued to share in the skimmed proceeds without interference from the new owners. This arrangement continued until around 1983, when indictments were issued against the Argent conspirators. Allen Glick was out of the gambling business, but he and his sons were still alive.

Around the same time in 1978 that Glick was initially approached about selling Argent, the feds launched a major investigation into organized-crime's influence in Las Vegas. A large part of that effort consisted of court-authorized electronic surveillance of telephones and locations in Kansas City, Las Vegas, Chicago, and Milwaukee. The residences of Carl DeLuna, Anthony Civella, and Anthony Chiavola, Sr. were monitored. The business offices of Allen Dorfman, Joe Lombardo, Milton Rockman, and Angelo LaPietra were listened in on. Frank Balistrieri's office and a restaurant he owned were also bugged. The investigators learned a lot and conducted several court-authorized raids based on that information.

The Feds Hit Paydirt

Agent Gary Magnesen was working in Milwaukee then and recalled the information that was obtained on Frank Balistrieri.

"We'd been running the taps on Frank [Balistrieri] for close to a year. In one of the calls Frank made from his office, he mentioned that it was almost time for his 'transfusion.' We didn't know what that meant at the time, but later on, when we compared notes with our Kansas City office, it was determined that 'transfusion' referred to the money coming in from the Las Vegas casino skim.

"In March 1978, we had enough probable cause to get a search warrant and went to Balistrieri's house to execute it.

We had to break the door down with a sledgehammer to get in. Once we were inside, I told Frank that there wouldn't be any more 'transfusions.' He looked at me and realized that we knew about the skim. I could see the confidence drain out of him. He knew it was over."

The search that was perhaps most devastating to the criminals occurred on February 14, 1979, Valentine's Day. Federal investigators entered the home of Carl DeLuna and seized addresses, phone books, papers, and other documents. Among them were DeLuna's detailed records of the skim. They included the dates and nature of meetings and conversations among the conspirators, telephone numbers, and the disbursement of funds from the skimming operations. The evidence gathered represented a bonanza for law enforcement—and doom for the mobsters.

The records available to investigators placed the estimate of the money taken from the Stardust and Fremont casinos at well over $2 million. Former Cleveland underboss Angelo Lonardo testified before the Senate Committee on Government Affairs on April 4, 1988. At that time he was serving a prison sentence of life without parole, plus 103 years, for his role in operating the family's drug ring. He began his statement by highlighting his long criminal history, including a couple of murders he had committed. He later explained how the Las Vegas casino skim operated after his family became involved.

"The skim of the Las Vegas casinos started in the early 1970s. Starting in 1974 I began receiving $1,000 to $1,500 a month from the family through Maishe [Milton] Rockman. I did not know where the money was coming from, but I suspected that it was from the Las Vegas casinos. I learned this from various conversations I had with Rockman.

"Lefty Rosenthal ran the skim operation in Las Vegas. Rockman would travel to Chicago or Kansas City to get Cleveland's share. Bill Presser [a Teamster power broker and father of future Teamster president Jackie Presser] and Roy Williams received about $1,500 a month for their role in the skim. The Cleveland family received a total of about $40,000 a month."

By 1983, the government's case against the gangsters was ready to move from the investigative to the prosecutorial stage. On September 30, a federal grand jury in Kansas City returned an eight-count indictment against 15 defendants in the Argent case. Five of them eventually stood trial, starting in late 1985: Chicago boss Joe Aiuppa, underboss John Cerone, West Side honcho Joe Lombardo, Milton Rockman, and Angelo LaPietra. Four of the accused, Carl Civella, Peter Tamburello, Anthony Chiavola, Sr., and Anthony Chiavola, Jr., entered guilty pleas prior to trial. Carl DeLuna and Frank Balistrieri pled guilty during the trial. Two others, John and Joseph Balistrieri, were acquitted. One, Carl Thomas, had his indictment dismissed during the trial and became a witness against the other defendants. And one, Tony Spilotro, had his case severed from the others prior to trial.

Other key players in the scam also testified during the trial. Allen Glick, Angelo Lonardo, and Roy Williams provided crucial evidence that resulted in guilty verdicts against Aiuppa, Cerone, Lombardo, LaPietra, and Rockman in January 1986.

Aiuppa and Cerone each received sentences totaling 28½ years. Lombardo and LaPietra drew 16 years in prison. Rockman got 24 years behind bars. In addition, each man was fined $80,000.

The Tropicana

This case also involves the Teamster pension fund. But unlike Argent, it was a loan *not* granted that paved the way for Kansas City to take control of the casino and launch another skimming operation. It began in 1975 when Joe Agosto, an affiliate of Nick Civella's Kansas City family, made a move to gain influence at the Tropicana.

Agosto was born Vincenzo Pianetti in 1927. Information on his early years is vague. There are even conflicting reports as to exactly where he was born, whether in Italy or Cleveland. Whichever the case, Agosto ended up in Seattle and eventually Las Vegas. He got his foot in the door at the Trop by assuming the title of manager of the *Folies Bergère* show. The hotel didn't employ him, however; he was an employee of the production company.

That April, the U.S. Immigration Service arrested Agosto as an illegal alien. He quickly obtained the services of Oscar Goodman and beat the immigration charge. Clear of that, he began conspiring with Nick Civella on how he could best infiltrate the financially troubled casino and protect himself from outside interference. Agosto, with Civella's backing and support, proceeded with his plans to gain influence over the Doumani brothers, owners of the Tropicana. In conjunction with that goal, a loan application by the Tropicana pending before the Teamster Central States Pension Fund was denied, easily delivered by Civella's friend Roy Williams. With their financial lifeline off the table, the Doumanis were susceptible to Agosto's overtures and he soon had a voice in the Trop's management and operations.

Agosto maintained regular contact with Carl DeLuna in order to provide reports on his progress and receive guidance. Kansas City, meanwhile, had a man they felt was able to set up and operate the skim. Carl Thomas was already licensed through his operation of the Bingo Palace and Slots-A-Fun casino, and was trusted by the Civella family. Following instructions, Agosto brought Thomas on board.

But late that year before the skim got off the ground, a snag developed that stalled the gangster's plans for over two years. The cash-strapped hotel came under the control of a new majority owner when chemical heiress Mitzi Stauffer Briggs purchased 51% of the Trop's stock. And right off the bat, Mitzi didn't trust Agosto and curtailed his role in running the casino. That prompted an all-out effort by Agosto to gain her confidence. By 1977, he had succeeded and was effectively running the hotel and casino. Carl Thomas did his duty and designed the skim. At his suggestion, Agosto hired Donald Shepard as casino manager and Billy Caldwell as assistant manager.

In March 1978, Agosto and Thomas spoke with Nick Civella in Los Angeles. They announced that with their plans and personnel in place, they were ready to go. Civella gave his approval. The first $1,500 dollars was skimmed in April by Shepard and transported to Kansas City by Carl DeLuna. In May, Shepard hired Jay Gould as cashier to steal money directly from the cashier's cage and falsify fill slips to account for the missing money. From June through October, Shepard, Caldwell, and Gould stole $40,000 per month and gave it to Agosto. The money was then passed on to a courier named Carl Caruso for transport to Kansas City. Caruso turned the loot over to Civella's man, Charles Moretina.

Caruso made at least 18 trips between Las Vegas and Kansas City and was paid $1,000 after each delivery. Anthony Chiavola, Sr., Civella's nephew and a Chicago police officer, assisted in the operation by getting Chicago's share of the skim to Joe Aiuppa and underboss John Cerone.

The operation seemed to be perking right along, but in late September another potential problem arose. Agosto and the Civellas became suspicious that Shepard or his subordinates might be doing some unauthorized skimming. At Agosto's suggestion, Nick Civella ordered the skimming suspended in November and December so that Carl Thomas could find out if someone was skimming the skim. Unfortunately for Agosto, Civella authorized a temporary halt in the stealing, but not in the payments to Kansas City. Since the problems had arisen on his watch, Agosto had to send the family $50,000 and $60,000 of his own money during the two months of downtime. But it wasn't a total loss for Joe. He was later reimbursed $30,000, which Shepard pilfered from the Tropicana.

On November 26, Agosto and Thomas flew to Kansas City to meet with the Civellas and DeLuna. They explained that Thomas' survey had been inconclusive, but they did have some ideas on improving the efficiency of the operation. Civella agreed that the skimming would resume in January.

The conspirators were unaware at the time that their homes and businesses were the subject of electronic and visual surveillance by the government. On February 14, 1979—the same day Carl DeLuna's home was raided—the FBI nabbed Caruso with $80,000 in skim money. The skimming of the Tropicana was over. Although the actual skim only occurred over a period of 11 months, during two of which the operation was suspended, the overall conspiracy to steal from the casino covered four years, 1975 to 1979.

Nick Civella had an even more serious problem than the Tropicana investigation. The Kansas City boss had been convicted in 1975 on gambling charges unrelated to Las Vegas. After exhausting his appeals, he went to prison in 1977. He was given an early release 20 months later due to health problems: He had cancer. Shortly after getting out, he was indicted again for attempting to bribe a prison official in an effort to get favorable treatment for his nephew, who was incarcerated. Convicted in July 1980, he was sentenced to a four-year stretch. So Nick was already behind bars in November 1981 when he and 10 others were indicted in the Tropicana case. His lawyer in that matter—Oscar Goodman—successfully got the charges against Nick severed from the other defendants on the basis of his client's poor health. On March 1, 1983, with his physical condition rapidly deteriorating, Civella was released to his family so he could spend his final days at home. He died on March 12, having never faced justice in either the Tropicana or Argent cases.

The 10 remaining defendants stood trial in 1983. Three

of them, Donald Shepard, Billy Caldwell, and Joe Agosto, entered guilty pleas prior to trial. As a part of his plea arrangement, Agosto became the government's key witness. Carl Caruso pled guilty during the trial. Peter Tamburello was acquitted. Carl Civella, Carl DeLuna (represented by Oscar Goodman), Charles Moretina, Anthony Chiavola, Sr., and Carl Thomas were all convicted.

In a memorandum to the judge regarding the case, prosecutors wrote, "These defendants have dealt a severe blow to the state and the industry and have made a mockery of the Nevada regulatory procedures." At sentencing the judge dealt a severe blow to the defendants.

DeLuna was sentenced to 30 years, Civella got 35 years, Moretina was ordered to serve 20 years of incarceration followed by five years of probation, and Chiavola drew 15 years. Carl Thomas was initially sentenced to 15 years. That term was later reduced to two years when he agreed to be a cooperative government witness at the Argent trial.

Joe Agosto died shortly afterward of natural causes. As far as is known, neither the Doumani brothers nor Mitzi Briggs were aware of the skimming operation. Mitzi Briggs later went bankrupt.

The ensuing appeals filed by those convicted in both the Tropicana and Argent cases were unsuccessful.

Following the Money

While FBI agents and prosecutors from several offices participated in the investigations that brought down the mobsters and ended organized-crime's hidden control over the Las Vegas casinos, personnel assigned to Sin City itself played a major role, albeit with one rather embarrassing moment.

The agents were confident that casino money was leaving Vegas illegally and ending up in Chicago, but they needed to prove it. The feds placed the Stardust and certain employees under physical surveillance. After months of investigation, they identified a pattern for one method of the skim involving Allen Glick's Stardust and Fremont casinos. Their big break came in May 1981.

"One of the people we were watching was a guy named Bobby Stella," former agent Emmett Michaels remembers. "One Tuesday afternoon my partner and I saw Stella leave the casino carrying a brown paper bag. We followed him to the parking lot of a hardware store on Maryland Parkway. This particular business had several locations in Las Vegas. A man identified as Phil Ponto, who was also employed by the Stardust, met Stella there. We found out later that Ponto was a 'made man,' affiliated with the Chicago Outfit. The two talked for a few minutes, then Stella passed the bag to Ponto and drove away. We stayed with Ponto and the bag."

Ponto left the hardware store and drove to his home, located off Paradise Road near the Las Vegas Hilton. He went into his house, but emerged a few minutes later to retrieve the bag from his car. The surveillance continued, but there was no activity of importance the rest of the week. Things changed on Sunday, though.

"Ponto left his house around 7:30 that morning and placed the brown bag in the trunk of his car. For some reason he then moved the car across the street, and then went back inside," Michaels continued. "He came back out a few minutes later and drove to church. After mass he drove around town for two hours with no apparent destination or purpose. He drove in and out of shopping malls and parking lots, but made no stops. Eventually, he pulled into another one of the hardware store locations; this one was on Tropicana. There he made contact with another man we weren't familiar with. The new guy was wearing a suit and driving a rental car. They talked for a few minutes, and then Ponto handed the bag over to the new guy. We dropped Ponto and followed the stranger as he headed toward California on Interstate 15."

With the agents watching, the guy in the rental car pulled into the second rest area outside of Las Vegas. There, he emptied bundles of money from the paper bag and placed them in special pockets sewn into the inside of his suit coat. When all the money had been transferred, the courier continued on to the Los Angeles airport where he caught a flight to Chicago. Agents from southern Nevada contacted the Chicago FBI office, asking agents there to pick up the surveillance of the subject when his flight arrived. After reaching Chicago, the man paid a visit to Outfit boss Joe Aiuppa, presumably to deliver the money. The courier was subsequently identified as Joseph Talerico, a Teamster official.

The agents had validated their theory of the skim, but they were a long way from having proof that would stand up in a court of law. Additional investigation indicated that money was also being skimmed from the Glick-controlled Fremont. The G-men believed the cash was taken from there on a monthly basis and delivered to Chicago. They developed a plan that called for the lawmen to get marked money into the skim pipeline. That meant agents would have to visit the Fremont the evening before a suspected shipment and do some gambling at the tables. Emmett Michaels, Charlie Parsons, and Michael Glass were tasked with getting the marked money into the system. In order to get a sufficient number of $100 bills into the drop boxes, they had to lose.

"I always had trouble losing when I was playing with government money," Emmett Michaels recalled with a grin. "I played blackjack and often had some incredible runs of good luck. Sometimes I'd be so desperate to lose that I'd have to buy more chips, that I'd play very recklessly. I'd throw even the most basic strategy out the window and call for a hit on a hand of nineteen. The dealer and the other players would look at me like I was crazy. But when I was on one of those streaks, I'd draw a damn deuce."

Sometimes that kind of luck drew attention that wasn't

necessarily wanted. "There were times when I'd have stacks of chips piled up in front of me and the pit boss would come over and invite me to get some of the perks reserved for high rollers. It was usually a different story when I was spending a night out somewhere else and playing with my own money."

In spite of his undesired prowess at the table, Michaels and his colleagues were able to drop enough money to accomplish what they wanted to do. Now that they knew their plan would work, the next step was to choose a time when the courier would be picked up and nabbed with the proof of the skim in his possession.

The Cookie Caper

In order to conduct electronic surveillance and searches and to make arrests, a judge had to approve and sign warrants. Some of the lawmen involved suspected that a certain judge might not be keeping the FBI's operations a secret. They found it hard to believe, for example, that after bugging a table in a Stardust restaurant where the casino manager and assistant manager ate their meals every day, the only things the men seemed to talk about were golf and women. But the government was required to follow the law and obtain the appropriate warrants and authorizations regardless of their suspicions.

"Harry," a bail bondsman who came to Las Vegas in 1958, thinks he knows another method of how the bad guys found out about whose phones were being tapped. "I had a lot of juice with the phone company then. I know for a fact that a phone-company employee regularly provided a list of numbers that were going to be tapped. I know because I received a copy of those lists myself. There were a lot of people very glad to get that kind of information."

In addition to the phone-company employee, Harry alleges there was an even better source for leaks. "There was a concern at the phone company that a phone might be tapped without having full legal authorization. So the company hired a lawyer to review all the paperwork for each tap. It turns out that the lawyer they retained worked out of Oscar Goodman's office. Did you ever hear of anything so outrageous?"

Whether leaks resulted as Harry contends, were the work of an unscrupulous judge, or a combination of both, the bottom line is that the targets frequently knew ahead of time what the lawmen were planning.

Stan Hunterton, the former Strike Force attorney, was involved in preparing and submitting warrant applications to the court and helping plan some of the law-enforcement activities, including when arrest warrants would be served.

"Joseph Talerico was always the courier for the skim money from the Argent casinos," Hunterton recalled. "The routine was for him to come to Vegas and get the money. His contact here was Phil Ponto. This Ponto was what we called a sleeper. That's someone with no criminal record, but Ponto was actually a 'made man' out of Chicago. One of the agents thought he recognized Ponto's name from a book written by mobster-turned-informant Jimmy Fratiano. It turned out the agent was right, only in the book the name had been mis-spelled as Ponti.

"On January 3, 1982, not long after the indictments in the Tropicana case, the FBI was ready to arrest Talerico and Ponto when they exchanged the skim money. The day started off with a variation on the part of Ponto; he was carrying a box instead of a paper bag. I guess everybody assumed they'd decided to put the money in a box that day and didn't think too much of it. But when the arrests were made, there was no money. The box contained cookies and wine.

"It was obvious that the bad guys had become aware of what was coming down. They had set us up, no doubt about it. I can smile about it all these years later, but I can assure you there was nothing funny about it at the time. An awful lot of time and effort had been spent getting to that point, and then it all went down the toilet. Needless to say, we were the butt of a lot of jokes in what became known as the cookie caper."

Hunterton hauled Talerico and Ponto before a grand jury in 1983. Their first effort to avoid talking was to exercise their Fifth Amendment rights against self-incrimination. Hunterton countered that by granting both men immunity. Even with no legal reason to remain silent, the pair still refused to testify. They were each sent to jail for contempt, but their lips remained sealed. They never did answer the government's questions.

Strawman case agent Lynn Ferrin remembers the skimming investigations very well. "They were exciting times," he said.

"When we were watching Ponto and Talerico, we made high-quality films of their meetings. On one occasion we brought in three lip readers to try to figure out what their conversations had been. One of the experts came very close to what we believed had been said; we would have loved to be able to use his interpretation in an affidavit. But the other two had differing opinions. With that lack of agreement, we ended up disregarding all of their versions. I even rented an apartment next to Ponto's residence for a while during the surveillance. I spoke with him occasionally. He was very quiet … a real sleeper."

Regarding the cookie caper, "It was a real bad day for us and me personally. If I'd been living in feudal Japan I'd have been required to fall on my sword. We'd been doing these Sunday surveillances on those guys for several months and everything had always gone like clockwork. But on that day the crooks were so confident and comfortable; we'd never seen anything like that before. We didn't know for sure who, how, or why, but someone had obviously ratted us out to the mob. We were highly confident that the leak wasn't from any of our people. Many of us believed that the federal judge who signed the order authorizing the electronic surveillance at the Stardust was the culprit. That was only speculation, but after that it seemed like the bad guys were aware of what we were doing. We had to call Washington and tell them what happened and that we couldn't say for certain why it had gone wrong.

"Prior to that day I had been in favor of simply stopping Ponto one of those mornings and grabbing the bag from him. He certainly couldn't have complained to the police and it would have given us the probable cause we were looking for. But headquarters and DOJ [Department of Justice] were afraid something would go wrong and never approved the snatch. If they had, it would have caused a lot of ripples in the various crime families. They may have even taken action against some of their own if they suspected them of being involved in stealing the skim."

Another incident that Ferrin described as "sensitive" involved aerial surveillance. "Our plane developed some problems and was forced to land on the golf course at the Las Vegas Country Club. It turned out to not be a very discreet surveillance." This scene was depicted in the movie *Casino*.

But other covert operations went very well. "Our guys did a tremendous job. Agents posing as maintenance men bugged a table in a restaurant at the Stardust in front of a room full of guests and casino employees. It was a good placement."

After the cookie caper, the FBI changed tactics from covert to overt and went after the Stardust's new owners, the Trans Sterling Corporation, openly. "We had enough information to start going over their records," Ferrin said. "The Carl Thomas method of the skim primarily involved stealing from the count room. We found that another method of theft was also going on at the Stardust. This one involved the cashier's cage.

"We looked at thousands of fill slips from the Stardust for the years that we knew the skim was going on. The fill slips were used when chips were removed from the cage to replenish the supplies at the gaming tables when they ran low on chips. The slips were required to have the signatures of four different casino employees. The money involved was about $20,000 per slip, and was presumed to reflect [casino] losses at the tables. We eventually discovered a pattern of forged signatures on the fill slips. That discovery led to the next step. We took handwriting samples from over two hundred Stardust employees and sent them to the FBI lab in Washington. Analysis revealed that the casino manager, Lou Salerno, was responsible for most of the forgeries.

"We got some good convictions in this phase. More important, though, through our investigation we were able to help the Nevada Gaming Control Board seize the Stardust. They revoked the licenses of the Trans Sterling people and fined them $1 million. The Stardust was eventually purchased by the Boyd Group, ending over a decade of mob control."

That wasn't the entire story for Lynn Ferrin, though. "The cage manager was a guy named Larry Carpenter. During the course of the investigation, he came to hate my guts. We lived in the same neighborhood and some mornings I'd come out to go to work and find that someone had spit all over my car. I'd have to clean the car off before heading for the office. I suspected that Carpenter was responsible.

"Carpenter was gay and had full-blown AIDS. I thought maybe he was trying to infect me by having me come in contact with his body fluid and absorb it through my skin. Anyway, I stayed up all night to see if I could find out who was sliming my car. Around 5 a.m. I caught Carpenter coming around the corner on his bike. I could tell by the look on his face that he was the one. It never happened again after that morning. Carpenter later committed suicide, hanging himself when he went to jail."

But there was more. "Lou DiMartini was a floorman at the Stardust. He claimed that during the investigation I caused him to suffer irreparable harm by asking his employer questions about him. He filed a $1 million civil suit against the government and me individually. It took seven years and the case went all the way to the U.S. Supreme Court where it was decided in the government's and my favor."

How does Ferrin sum up the results of the Strawman investigations?

"I think that our investigation basically broke the back of the mob's efforts to control the casinos in Las Vegas."

That last statement seems to say it all.

13

Time Running Out

As his cohorts in the Midwest went to prison or died, Tony Spilotro remained alive and free. But the sand in the hourglass was beginning to run out for him. Tony and Oscar Goodman had won a mistrial in the first Hole in the Wall Gang trial when two jurors were heard discussing something to do with money during a break outside the courtroom. Although this technicality gave the Ant a temporary reprieve, it did nothing to improve his chances for acquittal when the case was finally heard. A new trial was scheduled to begin on June 16, 1986.

The evidence against the Bertha's burglars was overwhelming. Spilotro's strongest argument would be that he wasn't present at the scene, leaving it up to turncoats Frank Cullotta and Sal Romano to implicate him in the burglary. Perhaps Goodman would be able to come up with another miracle and get his client off one more time. The odds were against it, though.

Two other cases were hanging over Spilotro's head as well. He still had to face the Argent charges and, based on the verdicts against the other defendants, it didn't look good for him.

And the Lisner murder of 1979 had yet to be resolved.

As though Tony didn't have enough problems, he also came under investigation for allegedly attempting to bribe a caterer into poisoning members of a sitting grand jury. Nothing resulted from the investigation and it didn't get a lot of ink. But it did serve to enhance Tony's reputation as a dangerous killer and that's not the image a defendant wants in the minds of potential jurors.

Tony and the Media—Ned Day

In addition to law-enforcement's efforts to get the best of Spilotro through the legal system, those familiar with the situation believe that the intense media coverage Tony received was instrumental in his eventual downfall.

Bob Stoldal, News Director at KLAS-TV, believes his station was the leader among the electronic media in their Spilotro reporting. "In the early days we had three reporters who did the primary reporting on Spilotro. They were Ned Day, Gwen Castaldi, and George Knapp. They were very aggressive in gathering and reporting information."

Ned Day in particular proved to have the ability to get under Tony's skin. Day moved to Las Vegas from Milwaukee in 1976 and took a job as a reporter with *The Valley Times* newspaper. Bob Stoldal subsequently hired him at KLAS. While there, Day moonlighted as a columnist for the *Review-Journal*.

"Ned developed the reputation of being a man of his word. If you shook Ned's hand on something, you had a deal. In that regard, he was respected by politicians, entertainers, and organized-crime figures alike," Stoldal said. "In Tony's case, when Ned reported on him either on the air or in print, he invariably referred to him as 'the Ant.' Ned had an idea Tony wasn't particularly pleased about that, but he made it a point to use the term regularly. Just in case Tony got too upset, when we went to a mob bar for a drink, we'd order unopened bottles of beer and glasses. We carried our own bottle opener with us to be on the safe side."

Former Sheriff John McCarthy shares Stoldal's opinion of Ned Day as a straight shooter. "I had a great deal of respect for Ned. On occasion he would strip some bark off me, but for some reason I wasn't offended. Ned was always professional and had a great sense of humor."

All the pressure was having an impact on Tony emotionally and physically. He was spending an increasing number of mornings staying in bed with the covers pulled up over his head. And the news media kept the attention on him. The persistent Ned Day had a number of reliable FBI and Metro sources and not only generated news about the gangster, but he also made fun of him at times. The reporter's articles didn't always sit well with Tony.

On the serious side, Day wrote a biting piece in the *Review-Journal* after Spilotro was acquitted of the M&M murders, had evidence in other cases thrown out on technicalities, and delayed other trials on procedural issues. The headline was, "How Can Spilotro, Incredibly, Still Walk the Streets?" That column read in part:

"Take, for example, the case of Tony Spilotro, the stubby kahuna of the Las Vegas streets. He still struts around town, despite a decade of government charges that he commands a cutthroat gang of burglars, arsonists, extortionists, leg breakers, and other career terrorists.

"If things go according to form, it'll be 1990 or beyond when his second case goes to trial.

"But what about the rights of society, the rights of law-abiding citizens who want justice? How many burglaries, thefts and extortion schemes can be carried out by a group of career criminals in the next eight years? How many victims will there be?"

Day's humor was evident in another *Review-Journal* piece

in March 1986. On that occasion he lamented that Spilotro might finally end up in prison. "Tough Tony Behind Bars: A Columnist's Disaster," read the tongue-in-cheek headline. In the column, Day pleaded with Oscar Goodman to keep the gangster free so that his own journalistic career could continue to prosper. Following are excerpts from that article:

"So, lawyer Goodman, I made your important client my project. I learned everything I could about him. I wrote a lot about him. I wrote bad things.

"In retrospect, I may have gone too far—like the time I dubbed him the 'Fireplug Who Walks Like a Man.'

"The point is that thanks to Mr. Spilotro's presence in Las Vegas, my career as a newsman has been okay.

"I'm pleading with you. Please do everything you can for Mr. Spilotro. My career may be riding on it."

According to John L. Smith's *Of Rats and Men*, that particular Ned Day column caused Spilotro to lose his cool. When the reporter encountered Tony in a corridor at the courthouse, the irate gangster issued him a not very veiled threat. Smith cited a paragraph about the encounter that appeared in Day's column a few days later.

"'I heard you want to be famous,' Spilotro said, adopting a cold, steady stare that made me think being famous was not a good thing. 'I know how to make you more famous than you ever thought about. You know I know how.'"

Tony and the Media—Gwen Castaldi

Gwen Castaldi arrived in Las Vegas from Cleveland in 1974. Based on her experience as a reporter in Ohio, she quickly landed a similar position with KBMI News & Information Radio. She became News Director for KNEWS Radio in 1977. Bob Stoldal hired her at KLAS-TV later that same year. In 2004, she recalled her days as a reporter covering the mob in Las Vegas.

"Between 1974 and 1983 we saw probably the highest concentration of investigations, search warrants, affidavits, wiretaps, court appearances, Black Book hearings, and more on the mob-crackdown front. It was one occurrence after another ... major and minor ... a massive river of events and information flowing. There were super surveillances, snitches, backroom doings, dirty deals, raids, secret skims, and hidden ownerships. There was a constant cast of gritty characters, mouthy attorneys, and determined local and federal law-enforcement officers.

"It was a war of sorts, especially between U.S. Strike Force attorneys and the mob suspects and their lawyers. Political lives were impacted and caught up in the mess, too. No doubt some innocent lives got tangled up in those activities. And there's also little doubt but that some very guilty people got away. Some truths and secrets none of us will ever know.

"That period was an oddly fascinating, but tough and grueling time. It was probably the most weird complex chunk of time in organized-crime history. And it occurred on the open neutral turf of Las Vegas. I don't believe there was any other city where mob activity played out this way. That decade or so was definitely a major turning point that changed the face of Las Vegas gaming. It ushered out one era and brought in another. It holds many intense memories for those of us who covered it for the media or were involved from any angle ... law enforcement, or their targets and attorneys.

"Covering those seemingly never-ending stories consumed huge amounts of time from everyone's lives. Those years were, perhaps, the most unique and intriguing, but also distasteful, in recent Nevada history to observe and experience."

Tony and the Media—Andrea Boggs

Andrea Boggs worked as a news anchor and reporter for Las Vegas station KORK-TV (now KVBC) from 1975 to 1981. Covering the exploits of Tony Spilotro and Lefty Rosenthal were part of her duties. In February 2005 she shared her memories of those times.

"I was a newswoman, and one of my goals was to get an on-camera interview with Tony Spilotro. That would have been a major coup for me. I was never able to do it, but it wasn't for lack of effort," she said.

In her pursuit of that elusive interview, Andrea periodically stopped at Spilotro's jewelry store, the Gold Rush. Herb Blitzstein usually manned the counter at the store. He'd let the reporter inside, but her cameraman wasn't allowed through the door. Once admitted, Tony would or wouldn't talk to her, depending on his mood.

Spilotro had a fearsome reputation as a mob enforcer. Was she nervous when meeting with him?

"Tony always treated me with respect. I never had the feeling that he'd hurt me; I never felt threatened when I spoke with him at the Gold Rush or elsewhere. But as polite as he was, he wouldn't agree to an interview. He usually said that his lawyer, Oscar Goodman, wouldn't allow it. I think that was true, too. Oscar probably didn't want to take a chance that Tony might say something that could come back to haunt him, and have it be on film."

Although Goodman may have impeded Andrea's efforts to land a sit-down with Spilotro, the lawyer himself was great from a reporter's perspective.

"I can't ever remember Oscar Goodman turning down a request for a comment or interview. He always made himself available and tended to be quite animated. If you caught him right after an adverse ruling in court, you could almost see the steam coming out of him."

Tony Spilotro and Oscar Goodman weren't the only people Andrea was interested in talking with. Lefty Rosenthal and Allen Glick were also major players in Vegas at the time.

"I don't remember if I was able to get Lefty to agree to a formal interview or not. I know I did speak with him several times, frequently at the Stardust. That was the scene of a lot of the action in those days, and it was where I spent quite a bit of time. I was able to talk with both Lefty and his wife Geri.

"Lefty was always impeccably dressed. You might say he was a perfectionist when it came to his clothes. I thought Robert De Niro did a nice job of bringing that point out in the movie *Casino*. I got the sense from talking with Geri and others that Lefty was very possessive of his wife. He was in control to the point that he picked out her wardrobe. I believe she was intimidated by him to some degree."

Andrea was able to get the attention of her media competitors when her persistence was rewarded in the form of a face-to-face interview with Allen Glick, the boss of Argent Corporation and reputed front man for the Chicago Outfit.

"I asked Glick on camera if he was acting as a strawman for the mob or the Teamsters. He flatly denied the allegations," Andrea remembered.

Reporters need to work with law enforcement, too. What was her relationship with them?

"I think I had a good relationship with both the law and the alleged bad guys. And that required keeping in mind what my job was. I was responsible for reporting the news, not for putting anyone in jail or keeping them out. In order to do that job I, or any good reporter, need to have sources of information. And developing and keeping sources depends on credibility. If people feel they can't trust you, you're in trouble. I had to walk a fine line and not be perceived as being too cozy with either side. The people who talked with me knew exactly where I stood and where they stood. That's what made it work."

Tony and the Media—Jane Ann Morrison

Jane Ann Morrison is currently a columnist for the *Las Vegas Review-Journal*. During the Spilotro days she covered the federal courts for that newspaper. In October 2004, she shared her recollections about working as a reporter back then via a column that appeared in the *Review-Journal* on November 27, 2004. Following are some of her thoughts taken from that piece.

"Maybe because I'm a woman, maybe because I didn't call him Tony the Ant in news stories, maybe because I wasn't any threat to him, for whatever reason, Anthony Spilotro was consistently polite to me.

"My most vivid memory of the man inevitably described as 'reputed mob boss' was his 1983 'perp walk' in Las Vegas, not his first and not his last.

"With FBI agent Charlie Parsons at his side, a smiling Spilotro walked by me and Channel 8's George Knapp, who asked the 'any comment' question. When I followed up, Spilotro winked. I shrugged, uncertain about the social etiquette for such an occasion.

"Spilotro, arrested that January day on charges he murdered and tortured two men in Chicago 21 years earlier, seemed simultaneously annoyed and amused. He had the reputation as a cold-hearted killer of as many as 22 people, yet he went to his grave without being convicted of any violent crime (partly because witnesses disappeared).

"Aside from the perp walk, my most vivid memories of Spilotro involve cocktails and covering federal court hearings, where I found myself chatting with his wife, Nancy, about something we had in common: cats.

"The Spilotros had cats and so did I. It was sort of neutral ground. Sure, I wanted to ask her about her marriage to a man believed to be the Chicago mob's overseer of its Las Vegas interests, but we both knew she wasn't going to answer.

"From the perspective of a reporter covering FBI and IRS raids and countless court hearings, that period was one great news story after another. Murder, bookmaking, prostitution, burglary, home invasions, extortion, fencing stolen jewelry. Spilotro's pals were convicted of this and that. But Spilotro's only conviction cost him a $1 fine: for lying on a home loan application.

"About those cocktails. Twice, Spilotro sent drinks to my table.

"Once was at a restaurant-bar on Maryland Parkway he favored. A bunch of *Review-Journal* staffers and I stopped by to check it out. I was torn between mortification at being caught sightseeing at a mob hangout and slightly pleased at the delighted reaction from my newspaper pals when Tough Tony sent us a round.

"The second time, I was lunching with an FBI agent.

"Spilotro and the boys came in for lunch, recognized both of us, and sent over two glasses of wine. I gulped mine. The agent didn't touch his and said he was tempted to show his contempt by pouring the wine on the floor.

"Fortunately, he didn't, and when I left I walked to Spilotro's table and thanked him for the wine. After all, he'd been unfailingly courteous to me."

Cause for Concern

The media coverage Tony Spilotro was receiving wasn't lost on the Midwest mob bosses. Tony was a suspect in up to 25 murders, and with three high-profile trials pending, his name was likely to appear even more in the newspapers, not less. Some in the underworld even felt that Tony had a penchant for the spotlight and that the attention it drew may have been partly responsible for the Argent fiasco. So, contrary to some upbeat rumors and media reports that he was still in good stead in the Windy City, Spilotro was in trouble not only with the law, but also with the underworld bosses, including Aiuppa's replacement, Joe Ferriola. The Outfit's new head wanted to begin his reign by getting his house in order. As a part of that effort, he took a hard look at Tony and found reason to be concerned.

Would Spilotro, with his health issues and the government closing in on him, follow the likes of Fratiano, Cullotta, and Romano into the waiting arms of the authorities? He was certainly a man who literally knew where the bodies were buried. And even if he stayed true to his oath of Omerta, what kind of revelations might come out when the pending cases against him finally made it to the courtroom? If Nick Civella were still alive, he might have asked if Tony was "crazy."

Ferriola and his associates came to a conclusion: Tony's negatives now outweighed his value to the Outfit. The new boss decided it was time to tidy up his organization and remove any threat of what Spilotro might say or do.

Murder in the Midwest—The Death of Tony Spilotro

Tony's 41-year-old brother Michael was also associated with the Outfit. He lived and owned a restaurant on Chicago. In early June 1986, he was contacted by a Ferriola underling and asked to get in touch with Tony and have him come to Chicago for a meeting. The get-together was scheduled for June 14, two days before the start of the second HITWG trial in Las Vegas.

The Spilotro brothers left for their meeting on that day and were never seen alive again. Their battered bodies were found buried in an Indiana cornfield several days later. They'd been beaten senseless and there was some evidence that they may have been put in the ground while they were still breathing.

Tony Spilotro was dead at the age of 48. He had been involved in yet another murder that has so far remained unsolved—only this time it was his own.

A shocked Las Vegas news media informed its readers about the murders of Tony and Michael on Tuesday June 24. The *Review-Journal* ran the story on its front page. According to the Associated Press article, the Spilotro brothers were reported missing June 16 by Michael's wife, Anne, who said she last saw them June 14 at her suburban Oak Park home. A farmer discovered the two badly beaten bodies in a shallow grave on his Indiana cornfield on Sunday evening. The bodies had been identified as those of Anthony and Michael Spilotro, who had disappeared more than a week earlier.

The article described Michael, age 41, as a restaurant owner and part-time actor, who had been indicted in Chicago on extortion charges stemming from an FBI investigation of organized-crime links to prostitution. Authorities also said that the previous week a car in which the Spilotro brothers were reported last seen was found abandoned near O'Hare International Airport.

An Indiana State Police spokesman said the bodies, clad only in underwear, were buried one on top of the other in a five-foot grave. An examination of the bodies by a forensic pathologist indicated blunt-force injuries, probably caused by hands or feet, resulted in the deaths.

At a news conference in Indianapolis, the pathologist said the injuries "were about the head, neck, the chest, and to some extent, the extremities." He added that the bodies "had been in the grave for several days—at least a week and possibly longer." Due to the condition of the bodies, dental and fingerprint records were used to make the identifications.

Lawmen speculated that it was likely the killers didn't anticipate the bodies would be found so quickly, if at all.

The grave was about five miles from a farm owned by mobster Joseph Aiuppa, who was convicted in March on racketeering charges of skimming from a Las Vegas casino. Law-enforcement sources said there was no way to know if there was any connection between Aiuppa and the murders.

The news from Indiana wasn't totally unexpected in Las Vegas law-enforcement circles. In fact, some lawmen were surprised it hadn't happened earlier. Gene Smith expressed his feelings this way. "The department had been receiving intelligence that Tony's days were numbered. He'd been falling out of favor with the bosses for quite a while, because he wouldn't give up his street rackets and keep a low profile. But he was real tight with Joe Lombardo and that probably extended his life. When Lombardo and the others went to prison on the Strawman convictions, Tony lost his protection. He wasn't liked or trusted by the new regime and that sealed his fate. It was just a matter of when.

"As for Michael, the word was that he was running a protection racket without the approval of the Outfit and not cutting them in on the profits. There was also the possibility that if they only hit Tony, Michael might want revenge. The best solution for the boys in Chicago was to get rid of both of them at the same time."

Kent Clifford believes Tony himself, and law-enforcement's efforts against him, led to the murders. "Tony's ego and his ambitions caused most of his problems with the mob. By us [Metro] and the FBI keeping him in the news, he became too much of a liability. Either the law was going to put him away or the mob would take care of him. For Spilotro, those were the only two possible outcomes."

John McCarthy had foreseen the ending years earlier. "I predicted in 1981 that would occur. I couldn't believe that Tony's superiors would continue to tolerate his arrogance and in-your-face method of dealing with local authority. I felt that any day Tony would get whacked for attracting so much attention to the Outfit's activities. The only surprising thing about his violent end is that it took so long."

Ned Day conveyed his thoughts regarding Tony Spilotro's murder on June 25 in a *Review-Journal* column titled, "In Death, Sinister Tough Tony Spilotro Was Trivial." His conclusion was that after death, Tony became totally irrelevant.

"So tough little Tony Spilotro, the swaggering Las Vegas rackets boss, finally accepted the Chicago mob's version of an early retirement incentive program, clad in his underwear, his bloody head bashed in.

"This man, after all, had been as strong as they come on the streets, a hard-nosed thief; a ruthless extortionist; a steely-eyed killer who, cops say, took pride in murdering his victims in the most gruesome fashion possible.

"It seems somehow odd and anti-climatic that Tony Spilotro should rank in death as merely another bit of supporting evidence for a bunch of time-worn clichés—power corrupts; crime doesn't pay; live by the sword, die by the sword; you reap what you sow.

"For more than a decade in Las Vegas, when Tony Spilotro glared, men's knees buckled (they called it the 'death stare'), when Spilotro leered, women swooned.

"That's why it seems so odd that his mangled corpse now should appear so trivial, just another manifestation of old clichés, just another mobster dumped dead in an Indiana cornfield, or a trash compactor, or a car trunk—you've heard the story before.

"Now that he's gone, it's as if he never were."

A few days after this column appeared, Day's car was fire-bombed in the parking lot of his apartment building. Was that incident related to Day's less-than-flattering remarks about Tony Spilotro?

"There's absolutely no question that Ned was being sent a message. No question at all," Bob Stoldal said.

Mistaken Identity?

It's impossible to say how many people mourned Tony Spilotro's death, but to Vincent Spilotro, the news of his father's death was devastating; it was news that he didn't want to believe, and for a while he didn't. He convinced himself that due to the condition of the bodies when they were found, their identification had been bungled. In his mind, Tony wasn't dead at all. But eventually, even Vincent accepted the reality of the situation. His loving father, the man he adored, was gone forever.

No one was charged in the killing of the Spilotro brothers for nearly two decades, and Oscar Goodman doesn't believe there was a sincere effort at that time to solve the murders. He cites the fact that authorities didn't bother to interview him, a man with intimate knowledge of Tony Spilotro.

However, records show that the FBI did do a lengthy investigation in an attempt to identify and prosecute the killers. In a redacted report dated May 19, 1993, the FBI summarized the results of their investigation as follows:

"For information of the Bureau, in June of 1986, Anthony Spilotro, a known Chicago LCN (La Cosa Nostra) member and his brother, Michael Spilotro, a known LCN associate and suspected LCN member, were murdered and buried in an Indiana cornfield located at the outskirts of Enos, Indiana. Autopsies conducted showed that both Spilotros were beaten. The cause of death was listed for each as asphyxia, due to blunt forced trauma about the head, neck and chest. The bodies of the Spilotros were positively identified through dental records supplied by Patrick Spilotro, DDS, and brother of the two deceased.

"As in most gangland slayings, cooperation with law enforcement officials by associates and members of the Chicago LCN is virtually non-existent. Several cooperating witnesses and sources were developed in this matter and have provided the following information concerning the time and period just prior to the Spilotros disappearance and subsequent murders and events that followed the murders.

"Approximately 10 days before the murders, Anthony Spilotro arrived in Chicago, Illinois, with a female companion identified as (redacted), of (redacted), currently residing in (redacted). Information from (redacted) indicates that a meeting was scheduled between Anthony Spilotro and (redacted) on the date the Spilotros were last seen alive, June 14, 1986. On June 13, 1986, Michael Spilotro received two important phone calls from (redacted). After the second of these calls, Michael Spilotro was heard telling (redacted) that he had a meeting the next day. It is known from interviews conducted with (redacted) that (redacted) contacted Michael Spilotro at Hoagie's Restaurant during the evening of June 13, 1986. Hoagie's Restaurant was owned by Michael Spilotro. During the same evening, Michael Spilotro informed (redacted) that he had a meeting the next day with (redacted). Michael Spilotro said that if he didn't come back from that meeting, 'It's no good.'

"On June 14, 1986, Anthony and Michael Spilotro departed Michael's residence at approximately 4:00 p.m. and were never seen alive again. Prior to leaving the residence both Spilotros removed all valuables and identifying papers from their persons.

"It is speculated that the brothers met with associates they trusted implicitly and proceeded to the meeting place. Upon arrival at the meeting the Spilotros were beaten and strangled.

"Comments by (redacted) as well as (redacted) and confidential informants seem to indicate the following information regarding the murder of the Spilotro brothers:

"(redacted) and (redacted) participated in the murder of the Spilotro brothers.

"The Spilotro brothers may have been picked up at a motel in Schiller Park on the afternoon of June 14,

1986, by (redacted) and possibly (redacted). The last sighting of the brothers by witnesses was in the bar of the motel at approximately 3:00 p.m. Tony Spilotro's vehicle was later recovered at the motel parking lot. Because of the close relationship of (redacted) and Tony Spilotro, it is believed that the brothers may have voluntarily entered (redacted).

"It is believed that the six subjects beat the Spilotro brothers to death at a location believed to be near the burial site, located in Enos, Indiana. At least part of the reason for the killings was to get money from Tony Spilotro.

"Redacted paragraph.

"Redacted paragraph.

"Albert Tocco is currently serving a 200-year sentence on a conviction out of the Northern District of Illinois (NDI). An attempt was made to indict Tocco by a Newton County, Indiana, grand jury to enable the state prosecution of Tocco in a Newton County Superior Court, located in Kentland, Indiana. An Assistant United States Attorney (AUSA) from the NDI was to be cross-designated to handle the state prosecution of Tocco. The purpose behind the state prosecution of Tocco was to enable Tocco to receive a death penalty sentence, should he be convicted at the state level. It was hoped that this possibility for the death sentence would convince Tocco to cooperate in the Spilotro murder investigation. However, to date, there has been an inability to make arrangements for the payment of the anticipated high cost of this prosecution to be covered by federal funds.

"On November 2, 1992, Gary Shapiro, Criminal Chief, United States Attorney's Office, Chicago, Illinois, and David Capp, United States Attorney's Office, Northern District of Indiana, Dyer, Indiana, advised that they are both in agreement that at that time, there was no viable prosecution in either the Northern District of Indiana or Newton County, Indiana.

"Chicago Division is awaiting (redacted).

"Chicago will notify Headquarters upon the completion of the above and will then re-contact the United States Attorney's Office, NDI, for a final prosecutive opinion on this matter."

Based on the above document, it appears the FBI had a good idea of who was involved in the murders. It also seems that Albert Tocco, a long-time Outfit member, was a potential key witness. In spite of the information that had been gathered, the effort to charge and prosecute the slayers of the Spilotro brothers never came to fruition.

Former FBI agent Emmett Michaels received information on the Spilotro hits from what he considers reliable sources. His theory is partly supported by the FBI investigation. "Tony Spilotro was summoned to Chicago under the guise that he and his brother were going to be assigned by the mob to do a killing. It was not uncommon for men going out on a job to leave their identification and valuables at home. I believe the FBI report fits the scenario that the Spilotros thought they were going along on a hit. As it turned out, they were, but as the victims."

All the facts of what happened in Indiana that June may never be known and the murders might remain officially classified as unsolved. But the FBI is continuing to work the case and could at some point in the future develop sufficient evidence to name and/or prosecute the killers.

Tony Spilotro's death marked the end of an era in Sin City. The mob's hidden ownership and control of the casinos was ended; the "King of the Strip" was gone. The battle for Las Vegas was over, and the law had won.

14

Update

On April 25, 2005, federal indictments were announced charging 14 reputed members and associates of Chicago organized crime with running a decades-old criminal enterprise that was responsible for committing 18 murders. The slayings included those of Tony and Michael Spilotro.

Among those named as a result of the FBI-led investigation dubbed "Operation Family Secrets" was Joseph "The Clown" Lombardo. Mr. Lombardo was allegedly one of Tony's superiors during Spilotro's Las Vegas years. He was considered by many to have been a friend of the Spilotro family.

After nearly 19 years, how was this news received by some of those who knew Tony best? In order to find out, I reached three such people by telephone on April 25 and 26. Following are their comments.

Nancy Spilotro. "I'm thrilled. Absolutely thrilled." Tony's widow had been critical of the government's efforts to solve the killings of her husband and brother-in-law over the years. She explained: "I never said the FBI was doing nothing to solve the murders. But Tony and Michael weren't the Kennedys."

Regarding Joseph Lombardo. "I've known him like a cousin for forty years. But I'm going to withhold comment until I learn more details."

Vincent Spilotro. Although there had been rumors of indictments in his father's murder for some time, Vincent was pleasantly surprised when they actually happened. "I couldn't be happier," he said. In the weeks prior to the announcements, Chicago and Las Vegas reporters had contacted Vincent and his mother, hinting that major developments were pending and requesting interviews. No interviews were granted, however. The government gave them no prior warning of the indictments.

Frank Cullotta. Tony Spilotro's one-time friend and associate is not surprised at the news. "There were people around who knew what happened. It was a matter of getting someone to talk."

Cullotta's theory of why the two brothers were killed goes this way. Joe Ferriola, the new Outfit boss at the time (now deceased), and Joe Lombardo were behind the killings. "Tony had outlived his usefulness [to the Outfit] by causing too much heat in Las Vegas. Michael wasn't a made man, but he used his brother's reputation to run his own criminal activities in Chicago, including bookmaking. I think he made waves by roughing up one of Ferriola's bookies. On top of that, they [the Outfit bosses] knew that if they only hit one of them, the other would want revenge and there'd be a war. So they both had to go."

Another person quite familiar with the Spilotro case is Dennis Arnoldy, the former FBI Las Vegas case agent for the Spilotro investigations. On April 27, Mr. Arnoldy provided his comments.

"The orders to kill Tony and Michael likely came down from Joe Ferriola. Lombardo would have had little choice but to carry them out. Remember, when it comes to protecting the Outfit, its bosses, or business interests, there is no such thing as friendship or even blood ties. Even if Lombardo was a personal friend to Tony and Nancy, it would have made no difference."

Joseph Lombardo was not immediately arrested after the indictments were issued. Instead, he went into hiding and became a fugitive from justice. For nine months he avoided the law, but his luck finally ran out. On Friday, January 13, 2006, FBI agents nabbed him in Elmwood Park, Illinois, a Chicago suburb. As the charges against Lombardo and the other defendants move forward, perhaps the complete story of the demise of Tony and Michael Spilotro will be told.

15

Loose Ends

T his final section contains information on what happened to some of the key players in the book after Tony Spilotro's death in 1986. Not all of those persons are updated here. The primary reasons for these omissions are either the unavailability of useful information or the individual requested to be excluded.

Chicago

Joseph Ferriola, the man who allegedly ordered Tony Spilotro's execution, had only a three-year stint as boss of the Outfit. He died of natural causes in 1989.

Tony Accardo died in 1992 at the age of 86. Unlike many of his colleagues, he avoided serving any lengthy prison terms and his death was the result of natural causes.

Joseph Aiuppa passed away in February 1997. The 89-year-old was in prison at the time of his death as a result of his convictions in the casino skimming cases.

Las Vegas

The six members of the HITWG who were arrested for the Bertha's burglary were eventually prosecuted in Clark County, with their trials and pleadings occurring after Tony Spilotro's death. The dispositions of their cases, and their current status, are:

Wayne Matecki was found not guilty of burglary by a jury verdict. He is now living in Illinois.

Leo Guardino pled guilty to burglary and is now deceased.

Ernest Davino pled guilty to burglary. He is out of prison and residing in New Jersey.

Lawrence Neumann pled guilty to burglary. In 1983, while awaiting prosecution in the Bertha's case, he was convicted in Illinois of the 1979 murder of a Chicago jeweler. Frank Cullotta was the chief prosecution witness against Neumann at trial. The now 77-year-old is currently serving a sentence of life without the possibility of parole for that killing. He is housed in the state prison facility at Menard, Illinois, where he is known as prisoner number N33971.

Frank Cullotta pled guilty to attempted burglary. After switching sides and becoming a government witness, Cullotta testified at several trials and appeared before federal and state investigative bodies across the country. He currently operates a profitable small business, and is considered one of the success stories of the government's Witness Protection Program.

Mr. Cullotta also served as an adviser for the 1995 movie *Casino*, in which he made a cameo appearance. Near the end of the film there are several scenes in which potential witnesses against the mob are being eliminated. One of the murders depicted is identified as taking place in Costa Rica and involves a man being chased through his house and killed near the swimming pool. This incident was based on the 1979 murder of Jerry Lisner in Las Vegas, in which Frank Cullotta admitted to being the killer. He appeared in the movie re-creation as the shooter.

Joe Blasko, the former cop, served five years in state and federal prisons for his crimes while working with the Spilotro gang. He died of natural causes in November 2002, at the age of 67.

Oscar Goodman, the defense attorney who represented Tony Spilotro and several other alleged mobsters, was elected Mayor of Las Vegas in June 1999. He began serving his second term in April 2003 and has enjoyed high approval ratings while in office. Mr. Goodman often describes himself as "the happiest mayor in America."

Judge Harry Claiborne, who was a client of Oscar Goodman and the first federal judge in the nation's history to be convicted of criminal charges while sitting on the bench, committed suicide in January 2004 at the age of 86.

Spilotro lieutenant Herb Blitzstein was convicted of credit-card fraud in 1987 and received a five-year prison sentence. After his release in 1991, he decided to resume loansharking and fencing stolen property activities in Las Vegas. He was found dead in his Vegas townhouse in January 1997, shot execution style. Two men were arrested for the murder and pled guilty prior to going to trial. Two other men with ties to the Los Angeles and Buffalo organized-crime families were subsequently charged with hiring the hit men to kill Blitzstein so they could take over his illegal businesses. They were acquitted of those charges, but were convicted of running an extortion scheme to take over Herbie's loansharking and insurance-fraud operations. Blitzstein's death marked the passing of one of the last remnants of the Spilotro gang in Las Vegas.

Frank "Lefty" Rosenthal lives in Florida and is still involved with the world of sports betting. He has a sports-related Web site at http://www.frankrosenthal.com.

Ned Day, newsman and columnist, died in September 1987 while vacationing in Hawaii. An autopsy determined the

42-year-old died of a heart attack. Bob Stoldal, Day's boss at KLAS-TV and a personal friend, said he is "ninety percent sure" the autopsy report is accurate, but he continues to harbor an element of doubt about the findings. He believes that due to Day's frequent reports attacking organized-crime figures, foul play can't be completely ruled out.

News of the reporter's death sent shock waves throughout Las Vegas and beyond. He received accolades from his peers, politicians, crime figures and loyal fans, all expressing their respect and sadness over his passing.

Gwen Castaldi left KLAS in 1980. She began an 18-year career with KVBC-TV in January 1981, as a main anchor and reporter. In September 2003, she was hired by Nevada Public Radio as host and senior producer of KNPR's "State of Nevada" program. In November 2004, the highly successful show was expanded from a one-hour to a two-hour format. She and her husband left Las Vegas in 2005 and moved to Utah.

Ms. Castaldi also appeared in *Casino*, playing the part of a reporter interviewing the Robert De Niro character.

Vincent Spilotro, Tony's adopted son, remains in the Las Vegas area. For a period of time after his father's death, he was intent on getting revenge against the people who had murdered Tony. Drinking heavily, he planned to conduct his own investigation, identify the killers, and administer justice. He went so far as to stockpile guns and explosives to use against his father's enemies. Family members finally convinced him that retaliation was a bad idea and he abandoned his plans.

But his lifestyle led to other problems. Vincent experienced some serious health issues, including alcohol and substance abuse. He survived a bout with colon cancer, but is afflicted with pancreatitis and has chronic problems with kidney stones. His current health difficulties are not life threatening.

Nancy Spilotro, Tony's widow, is alive and well and still lives in the Las Vegas area.

The Feds

Joe Yablonsky, former special agent in charge of the Las Vegas office, is retired and living in Florida. He has written a manuscript about his stint in Las Vegas and is currently marketing it.

Charlie Parsons, the agent who visited Frank Cullotta in jail and informed him there was a contract on him, is the Executive Director and COO of the Drug Abuse Resistance Education (DARE) program, headquartered in Los Angeles.

Emmett Michaels, the electronics and surveillance expert who had exceptional luck when gambling with government money, is the Vice President of Corporate Security & Surveillance for Station Casinos, Inc.

Dennis Arnoldy, Las Vegas case agent for the Spilotro investigations, is a private investigator working for The Advantage Group in Las Vegas. He also operates a separate polygraph business as Dennis Arnoldy & Associates.

Lynn Ferrin, Las Vegas case agent for the Strawman investigations, is retired and lives not far from Las Vegas.

Stan Hunterton, former Strike Force attorney, has his own law practice in Las Vegas.

Las Vegas Metropolitan Police Department

Gene Smith is enjoying retirement and lives north of Las Vegas.

Gary Lang, LVMPD attorney, is practicing law in Las Vegas.

David Groover owns and operates a private investigative agency in Las Vegas doing business as David Groover & Associates, Inc.

Kent Clifford obtained a real estate license while working for Metro. After leaving the department he considered attending law school and an attorney had agreed to hire him upon graduation. As he was contemplating his future, he closed his first escrow on a vacant parcel of land. His commission on that one transaction was nearly what his potential employer had quoted him as an annual salary.

"At that time, I had a wife, three kids, and a dog all counting on me for support," Clifford remembered. "I decided to stay in real estate."

Today Clifford owns and operates Clifford Commercial Real Estate in Las Vegas.

John McCarthy moved to the Dallas, Texas, area in 1988, where he began a second career working as a civilian crime analyst for the Dallas Police Department. He retired in December 2004, at age 70.

Clark County District Attorney's Office

Jim Erbeck went on to prosecute organized-crime members as a federal prosecutor. In 1989 he was selected by President George H. W. Bush as United States Attorney for Nevada. He later operated a law practice in Las Vegas. He is currently semi-retired and living in New Jersey, where he cares for his elderly mother.

Mr. Erbeck views the 1982 conviction of Frank Cullotta, which made Cullotta receptive to law-enforcement initiatives to cooperate, as one of the highlights of his career. He also had this to say about his time in the Clark County DA's Office:

"Working with Gene Smith, Kent Clifford, Emmett Michaels, Dennis Arnoldy, Stan Hunterton, and especially Chief Deputy District Attorney Bill Koot were the most memorable and important things I ever did. It was an honor to work with Metro Intelligence, the FBI, and all those who were so committed to fighting the mob."

Index

ShopLVA.com
For Other Great Books on Las Vegas

Huntington Press is a specialty publisher of gambling- and Las Vegas-related books and periodicals, including the award winning newsletter *Anthony Curtis' Las Vegas Advisor*. Visit us on the Web at ShopLVA.com to view our complete selection of books about Las Vegas.

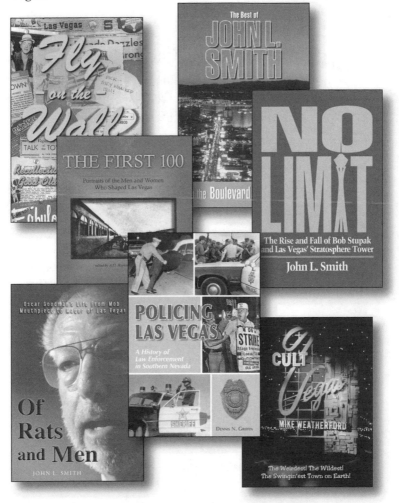

About the Author

Dennis N. Griffin retired in 1994 after a 20-year career in investigations and law enforcement in New York State. He and his wife Faith moved to Las Vegas shortly afterward. Dennis wrote his first novel, *The Morgue*, in 1996. He currently has six published mystery thrillers, including the first two books of a Las Vegas-based trilogy. The author is an active member of the Mystery Writers of America, Las Vegas Valley Writers Group, Henderson Writers Group, and the Police Writers Association. For more information, visit www.authorsden.com/dennisngriffin.